THE
PRESBYTERIANS

THE PRESBYTERIANS

RANDALL BALMER
and
JOHN R. FITZMIER

Foreword by Henry Warner Bowden

Westport, Connecticut
London

for our children,
Christian and Andrew
Daniel and Kathryn

The Library of Congress has cataloged the hardcover edition as follows:

Balmer, Randall Herbert.
  The Presbyterians / Randall Balmer and John R. Fitzmier.
    p. cm. — (Denominations in America, ISSN 0193–6883 ; no. 5)
  Includes bibliographical references and index.
  ISBN 0–313–26084–2 (alk. paper)
    1. Presbyterian Church—United States—History.   2. Presbyterian
Church—United States—Biography—Dictionaries.   I. Fitzmier, John
R.   II. Title.   III. Series.
  BX8935.B355   1993
  285′.1—dc20   92–17840

British Library Cataloguing in Publication Data is available.

An expanded, hardcover edition of *The Presbyterians* is available from the
Greenwood Press imprint of Greenwood Publishing Group, Inc. (Denominations
in America, Number 5; ISBN: 0–313–26084–2).

Library of Congress Catalog Card Number: 92–17840
ISBN: 0–275–94847–1 (pbk.)

First published in 1994

Praeger Publishers, 88 Post Road West, Westport, CT 06881
An imprint of Greenwood Publishing Group, Inc.

Printed in the United States of America

The paper used in this book complies with the
Permanent Paper Standard issued by the National
Information Standards Organization (Z39.48–1984).

10 9 8 7 6 5 4 3 2 1

CONTENTS

FOREWORD

The Praeger series of denominational studies follows a distinguished precedent. These current volumes improve on earlier works by including more churches than before and by looking at all of them in a wider cultural context. The prototype for this series appeared almost a century ago. Between 1893 and 1897, twenty-four scholars collaborated in publishing thirteen volumes known popularly as the American Church History Series. These scholars found twenty religious groups to be worthy of separate treatment, either as major sections of a volume or as whole books in themselves. Scholars in this current series have found that outline to be unrealistic, with regional subgroups no longer warranting separate status and others having declined to marginality. Twenty organizations in the earlier series survive as nine in this collection, and two churches and an inter-denominational bureau have been omitted. The old series also excluded some important churches of that time; others have gained great strength since then. So today, a new list of denominations, rectifying imbalance and recognizing modern significance, features many groups not included a century ago. The solid core of the old series remains in this new one, and in the present case a wider range of topics makes the study of denominational life in America more inclusive.

Some recent denominational histories have improved with greater attention to primary sources and more rigorous scholarly standards. But they have too frequently pursued themes for internal consumption alone. Volumes in the Praeger series strive to surmount such parochialism while remaining grounded in the specific materials of concrete ecclesiastical traditions. They avoid placing a single denomination above others in its distinctive truth claims, ethical norms, and liturgical patterns. Instead, they set the history of each church in the larger religious and social context that shaped the emergence of notable denomination features. In this way the authors in this series help us understand the interaction that has occurred between different churches and the broader aspects of American culture.

Each of the historical studies in this current series has a strong biographical focus, using the real-life experiences of men and women in church life to highlight significant elements of an unfolding sequence. Every volume singles out important watershed issues that affected each particular denomination's outlook and discusses the roles of those who influenced the flow of events. This format enables authors to emphasize the distinctive features of their chosen subject and at the same time recognize the sharp particularities of individual attributes in the cumulative richness that their denomination possesses.

The authors of this volume on *The Presbyterians* are not members of the denomination, and so they bring fresh perspectives allowed by that circumstance. They also bring to bear zealous work habits that they apply to a broad range of subject matter. Their topics range from intricate theological considerations in the Reformed tradition to institutional complexities for which Presbyterians are renowned on the local, as well as the national, level. Throughout their inclusive coverage they capture the essential characteristics of this denomination as it strove to affect secular culture with religious consciousness and moral standards.

As a large national body, Presbyterians have reflected their environmental conditions as much as they have had an impact on them. As a result, various segments of the denomination have embodied regional, sectional, socioeconomic, and gender preferences as the causes behind controversies, schisms, and reunions. Here, too, the authors trace accurate patterns to show how Presbyterians demonstrate American patterns of pluralistic differences and ecumenical ideals. These centrifugal and centripetal forces, blended with internal concerns about doctrine and worship, plus external considerations of influencing society at large—all combine to make Presbyterianism a crucial American denomination, and this volume an essential one in the series.

HENRY WARNER BOWDEN

PREFACE

In 1986 our friend Professor Henry Warner Bowden of Rutgers University approached us about the possibility of writing a volume in Greenwood's Denominations in America Series. This book is an abridged version of that volume. In hindsight, our response to Henry's proposal seems almost comic: Just out of graduate school, enthusiastic about the prospect of working together, and starstruck by Henry's assurance that a contract could be drawn up in a matter of days, we did what almost any young scholars would do—we promptly accepted his offer.

Our confidence, if not our enthusiasm, cooled soon after we began to appraise the task before us. This is a denominational history, written both for academics and for general readers who seek an informed and critical introduction to the Presbyterian tradition in America. It is narrative in form, not argumentative. Given the breadth of the Presbyterian tradition in America and the length limits imposed on volumes in the series, we had necessarily to craft a narrative that offered summary judgments and accurate overviews at the expense of detail. Thus, from the start we were working in a style and genre with which we had little experience.

To complicate matters further, the historical training and interests we brought to the project were not anywhere near an exact fit. Neither of us would describe himself as a denominational or institutional historian. Though we felt confident about our familiarity with the larger contours of American religious history, neither of us could claim particular expertise in Presbyterian materials. In fact, each of us was then contemplating the revision of studies on other subjects— Balmer's work on the social and religious interchanges between Dutch Reformed and Anglicans in the Middle Colonies, and Fitzmier's study of Timothy Dwight, the indefatigable New England Congregationalist.

Teaching and administrative tasks at Columbia University and Vanderbilt Divinity School also took their toll. And, as if to confirm what must have been

Henry's nagging suspicion that his invitation to us was clearly an error in judgment, neither of us could draw on personal affinities to the Presbyterian faith. This is *not* an insider's account of the Presbyterian tradition in America. We could not explain, for instance, why Presbyterians have this odd aversion to the use of articles when talking about their polity. They speak of being "elected to presbytery," rather than being "elected to *the* presbytery"; they go to assembly every year, not *the* assembly.

Although there were times when we wished for a sense of religious connection with our subject (the intimacy born of living within a tradition can, after all, provide good things for the historian—perspective, understanding, sensitivity, and empathy), in the end our distance from the subject of our research has seemed to us a good thing. Too often denominational history has suffered at the hands of sympathetic insiders whose critical edge has been blunted by their passion for their own brand of religious faith. We are not so naive as to claim historical "objectivity" in our work. Ironically, however, our appreciation of the internal dynamics, the remarkable durability, and the blessed diversity of American Presbyterianism actually grew as our work proceeded, even though we are still at a loss to explain the aversion to articles. We hope that such admiration has not dulled our historical wits.

This volume offers a narrative history of American Presbyterianism, from its origins in the Protestant Reformation, its development in Scotland and the American colonies, through the ecumenical movement of the twentieth century. Many of the names herein will be readily identifiable by anyone familiar with American Presbyterianism, but we have sought as well to recognize those less well known, especially women and people of color, whose contributions have often been overlooked.

Doubtless, some readers will find sins of omission and commission in this work. Fortunately, friends and students have alerted us to problems and have helped us to make corrections. Several students in the Graduate Department of Religion at Vanderbilt University deserve special thanks. David Roebuck lent us his organizational skills. William Evans, a knowledgeable student of Reformed theology, offered valuable insights on the thorny theological issues that are treated in Chapter 1. We are particularly indebted to Douglas Sweeney, who logged many hours of careful work on this project. He tracked elusive biographical details, read and commented on draft versions of the text, entered bibliographical citations on the computer, and spotted and corrected many infelicities—grammatical, theological, and historical. Without his work this project would have taken even longer than it has. Professor Henry Bowden, Professor Milton J. Coalter of Louisville Presbyterian Seminary, and Professor Stephen Crocco of Pittsburgh Theological Seminary read drafts of the narrative chapters of the volume. Henry's gentle admonitions about avoiding excess theological technicalia, Joe's deep knowledge of Calvin and his understanding of the contemporary scene, and Steve's reminder that the Presbyterian story transcends the mundane history of its internecine battles, have been of great help to us. Despite the guidance and advice of these colleagues, we take full responsibility for problems and errors that remain in the text.

Notwithstanding the debts we owe to our spouses, this book is dedicated to our children: Christian and Andrew Balmer, Daniel and Kathryn Fitzmier. They have grown and matured a good deal during the years we have worked on this project, and we reckon ourselves blessed to have been able to watch them do so.

Note: Asterisks next to various names throughout the text indicate that these individuals are the subjects of entries that make up the Biographical Dictionary which appears in the expanded hardcover edition.

THE
PRESBYTERIANS

1
REFORMED THEOLOGY AND THE DEVELOPMENT OF PRESBYTERIANISM

The story of Presbyterianism in America, like that of most American denominations, properly begins in sixteenth-century Europe. During the first decades of this epochal century, social, economic, political, and religious change accelerated rapidly. The foundations of European culture repeatedly shifted and realigned in response to these interconnected changes, leaving few of Europe's institutions untouched. One of the most powerful and important of these institutions, the Christian Church, would emerge from the century entirely transformed. The Reformation—both Protestant and Catholic—had begun.[1] Narrative accounts of the theological dimensions of the Reformation often commence with assessments of the "magisterial reformers"—Martin Luther, Huldrych Zwingli, and John Calvin—or with treatments of a host of other Protestant reformers such as Heinrich Bullinger, Martin Bucer, and Caspar Olevianus. Three of these reformers in particular, all of whom worked for the reformation of the churches in Switzerland, figure into the origins of American Presbyterianism.

Huldrych Zwingli was born in 1484. He was trained at Vienna and Basel in the humanistic tradition. He became a parish priest in 1506, and in the following decades he carefully followed the course of Martin Luther's struggles with Rome. In 1519 he was elected "people's priest" in Zurich, and within three years he became one of the canton's chief reformers. Zwingli engaged in public disputations, promoted liturgical reforms, preached almost daily, published theological treatises (the most famous of which was his *Commentary on True and False Religion*, published in 1525), and developed far-reaching and progressive political plans for Zurich. His political reforms evoked stiff resistance from his Catholic opponents and eventually led to armed conflict. When Zurich attempted to force Protestant reforms on Catholic cantons, war broke out and Zwingli was slain on a battlefield at Kappel in October 1531.[2]

Heinrich Bullinger, another humanist scholar who influenced the course of reform in Switzerland, was educated at Cologne. Like Zwingli, Bullinger's familiarity with Luther's protests against Rome drew him into the reform movement. Although the defeat of the Zurich reformers at Kappel and the death of Zwingli threatened the future of the Swiss reformation, Bullinger moved to Zurich shortly after the Kappel debacle, offered his services to his Protestant allies, and helped to stabilize the situation. Working toward unification among contentious Swiss Protestants, he was the principal author of the *First Helvetic Confession* and the *Second Helvetic Confession*, both of which became creedal cornerstones of the Swiss Reformation.[3]

The best known of the Swiss reformers was John Calvin. Born in Noyon, France, in 1509 and trained in theology and law, Calvin became persuaded of the need for ecclesiastical reform in his early twenties. In 1535, under the threat of persecution from the French Catholic monarch, Calvin fled to Switzerland. In Geneva, he worked with William Farel to reform local parishes. Although many Genevans accepted Calvin's early reforms, which regulated admission to the Lord's Supper and required citizens to make a profession of faith that was approved by the town council, his proposals concerning excommunication led to his exile in 1538. Calvin fled again—now in fear of Protestant wrath—to Strassburg, where he served as pastor to a French congregation. During this three-year exile, Calvin continued his theological writing and began work on a series of biblical commentaries that would earn him the nickname "the Prince of the Commentators."[4] Throughout the Strassburg exile and after his triumphal return to Geneva in 1541, Calvin the pastor, theologian, exegete, and politician helped give further shape to Reformed theology, a doctrinal system distinct from Roman Catholicism on one hand and from both Lutheran and Anabaptist Protestantism on the other.[5]

One of the guiding lights in the Reformed theological firmament was Calvin's *magnum opus, The Institutes of the Christian Religion*, which was edited, rearranged, and rewritten several times before it took its final shape in 1559.[6] It fills nearly fifteen hundred pages. By Calvin's death in 1564, the *Institutes* had become a standard textbook of Reformed theology on the Continent. American Presbyterians, for their part, would come to regard the *Institutes, The Westminster Confession of Faith* (1646), and Francis Turretin's *Institutio Theologiae Elenticae* as foundational theological documents in their tradition.

The *Institutes*, following the Christian confessional tradition of great antiquity, is arranged on a trinitarian model. The first three books of the *Institutes*—"The Knowledge of God the Creator," "The Knowledge of God the Redeemer," and "The Way in Which We Receive the Grace of Christ"—treat the roles of Father, Son, and Holy Spirit in salvation. The fourth book—"The Eternal Aids or Means By Which God Invites Us Into the Society of Christ"—describes the appropriation of that divine work. The *Institutes* was intended as an introduction to the themes of the Old and New Testaments. Although a host of doctrinal issues find thorough treatment in the *Institutes*, Calvin was not primarily interested in establishing the contours of theological orthodoxy and correct belief. Rather, his chief concern was with the faithful practice of Christianity and correct living.

As the title of one of the penultimate versions of the *Institutes* put it, the work concerned "the whole sum of piety." Undoubtedly this emphasis on personal religious experience as differentiated from (though not unrelated to) doctrine is one of the reasons for the enduring popularity of the *Institutes* within the larger Reformed tradition.

Reformed Protestantism, with roots reaching back to Bullinger, Zwingli, Calvin, and Farel, gave birth to a wide variety of diverse sub-traditions, only one of which was Presbyterianism. Members of the larger Reformed family have identified themselves in different ways: ethnically, nationally, on the basis of a unique doctrine, or by means of their particular organizational structure. What has united this international group of Protestants is a broad affirmation of the central tenets of Reformed theology, although that theology has been adapted to various social contexts, theological climates, and prevailing intellectual currents. Presbyterianism is but one part of this Reformed tradition.

REFORMED THEOLOGY

Reformed theology, like Calvin's *Institutes*, invariably has begun the task of theological reflection with single-minded attention to the doctrine of God. Even at this most fundamental stage of inquiry, however, the tradition has resisted the temptation to formulate an intellectual system that might be ill-equipped to guide Christians in everyday living. Reformed divines have acknowledged the essential connection between humanity's quest for the knowledge of God and its quest for the knowledge of itself. For them, the study of the divine leads to human self-knowledge, and, conversely, the study of humanity leads to the contemplation, if not saving knowledge, of the divine. This two-fold, reflexive enterprise has itself been grounded in a conviction that is at the very heart of Reformed faith, however. God is entirely independent, omniscient, omnipotent; God is, without exception, sovereign over all things.

Working from this central affirmation, Reformed theology has chronicled the progressive self-revelation of God down the long corridor of time. Gathering evidence of the activity of God from a series of living texts—the created order, secular history, the lives of the faithful, and the Bible—Reformed theology has narrated a long, often complex drama of God's grace toward humanity. Despite the complicated fabric of this narrative, and despite the different ways successive generations of Presbyterian and Reformed theologians have understood this narrative, several themes have consistently appeared.[7]

THE SOVEREIGNTY OF GOD

Precisely because God is entirely sovereign, Reformed theologians have stressed divine providence in salvation—that the redemption of humanity is initiated, sustained, and brought to its culmination by God's power and for God's glory. Given God's eternity, omniscience, and omnipotence, and in light of the scriptual teaching that salvation was part of the divine plan even prior to the foundation of the world, Reformed theologians have been forced to wrestle with the problem of predestination. Reformed theological reflection on this difficult doctrine—often caricatured as impersonal, abstract, "fatalistic," or unjust—admits of a rather stark and simple logic. Because God is entirely sovereign, and because humanity is sinful and incapable of unassisted moral and spiritual regeneration, God must be responsible for humanity's salvation. God initiated the plan of salvation, chose an elect people for salvation, redeemed them through Christ, and sanctified them with the Holy Spirit. This logic is reflexive, however; it not only accounts for the presence of the faithful, but can be made to explain the presence of the unfaithful. Again, precisely because God is sovereign, God is viewed as responsible—though not morally culpable—for the unbelief of non-Christians, be they atheists, agnostics, or adherents to other religions.

As one might predict, there have been varying interpretations of predestination within the larger Protestant tradition as well as among Reformed divines.[8] Calvin and the first generation of Reformed theologians embraced a double predestination scheme, like the one outlined above, whereby God positively chose some people for salvation—the elect—and others for damnation—the reprobate. This first generation of theologians, citizens of the sixteenth and seventeenth centuries, were led to these conclusions rather naturally; few of their contemporaries, either Protestant or Roman Catholic, questioned the idea that God damned sinners to hell. What distinguished Reformed thinkers was not that they believed that God punished sinners eternally. Rather, in contrast to their contemporaries, they believed that God had chosen some people for this fate prior to their birth and that God's choice depended entirely on the inscrutable divine will and in no way on human effort or merit.

Soon after the double predestination scheme began to be codified, however, theologians dissembled over several issues. Although few divines were prepared to oppose the notion that God was ultimately responsible for election, the idea that God actually destined some for damnation was deeply troubling. It seemed to lead to the conclusion that God was the author of sin, a notorious conundrum that had long plagued Christian theologians. The doctrine of double predestination also appeared to detract from human responsibility. Beginning in the seventeenth century Reformed theologians from several schools of criticism began to modify the double predestination scheme in an attempt to avoid the theological difficulties it posed. Simultaneously trying to uphold the doctrine of the sovereignty of God and yet avoid what seemed to be the logical implication of that doctrine—that God was busy damning part of creation—dissenters within the Reformed ranks proposed several alternative schemes.

Solutions to the dilemma ranged between two polar positions. On one extreme some Reformed theologians urged believers to uphold the sovereignty of God as a Protestant sine qua non. If this led to unsettling conclusions—that God foreordained sin, for example—so be it. As these conservative interpreters understood things, to make the sovereignty of God adiaphorous, a thing to be believed or not believed as one saw fit, was to slight God and endanger one's soul.

In the middle of the spectrum there developed several accommodationist theories that attempted to hold human freedom and divine sovereignty in a creative tension. One strategy aptly referred to as single predestination, argued that God actively chose only the objects of divine mercy from among the perishing mass of humanity; everyone else received the just desserts of their voluntary, sinful acts. Eschewing the tidy, logical symmetry of the double predestination scheme, the single predestination strategy changed the "baseline" of election. Faced with the fact that God could justly damn everyone, the idea that God might elect and save even one sinner seemed nearly incredible: In a universe governed by strict divine justice, mercy in any form became wonderfully exceptional. Although this strategy promised some relief regarding the problems related to reprobation, to some critics it appeared to be little more than a theological sleight of hand. For them, divine foreknowledge was the real issue; even if God did not positively decree damnation, God's omniscience implied that the divine mind understood the outcome of all such events in advance of their occurrence in time. Hence, for some, the single predestination scheme seemed to overlook or ignore God's omniscience.

On the opposite pole, however, other theologians protected the notions of human freedom, responsibility, and accountability, even if this meant that divine sovereignty had to be deemphasized. These thinkers identified uniquely human experiences—spiritual desire, acceptance, joy—as the central elements of the new birth or conversion. Divine activities—election, reprobation, and the logical conundrums that attended them—remained shrouded in mystery. Christian faith was seen in terms of the human experience of the divine presence, an experience that eluded facile cause-and-effect analysis. God's activity was considered necessary, but not sufficient to salvation. In light of the biblical tradition that required responsible moral action from women and men, and given the foundational conviction that the quests for the knowledge of God and of the self are different elements of a single enterprise, these scholars described the anthropological side of the matter, leaving the strictly theological matters open for speculation.

Perhaps the most creative of the attempts to reconcile divine sovereignty and human freedom issued in a sub-system within Reformed thought known as covenant theology. Given the nature of the doctrinal dilemma facing the tradition—somehow to conceive a system and language that could adequately describe the relations between divinity and humanity—it is not surprising that the notion of covenant found wide appeal. The covenant idiom was itself biblical, and because the covenant concept was fundamentally relational, it was flexible. The idiom could describe both the vertical relationship between humanity and God as well as horizontal relationships, in which peers voluntarily entered into conditional relationships with one another.

Taking the biblical accounts of creation as their starting point and borrowing heavily from medieval contract theory, Reformed exegetes examined the legal language of these narratives with increasing interest. To the Reformed interpreter it appeared that God, in the very context of creation, had struck a two-party contract or covenant with the primordial couple. The terms of the contract—its stipulations, the rewards for faithfulness, the punishments for unfaithfulness—were recorded with consummate care. God would give Adam and Eve dominion over creation, making them surrogate rulers of the world for all time, provided that they adhered to the terms of the covenant, not to eat of the tree of the knowledge of good and evil. If the stipulations of the covenant were disobeyed, the contract was broken and the aggrieved party would invoke the required punishments. This first covenant, dependent as it was on humanity's ability to act appropriately—in short, to work for its salvation—was denoted the Covenant of Works.

According to the biblical witness, however, the Covenant of Works was quickly violated. Adam and Eve disobeyed the commandment, and God, working entirely within the arrangements of the covenant, ejected them from paradise and invoked several ominous curses. But it was grace, not wrath, that the covenant theologians discovered as they further analyzed the narratives of the creation and the fall. The covenant paradigm, it seemed, had the capacity to describe both the fall of humanity and humanity's subsequent restoration to divine favor. Indeed, in the very act of cursing humanity for its profanation of the Covenant of Works, God promised that the progeny of Adam and Eve would ultimately triumph over evil. This progeny, called "the seed of the woman" in the text, would crush the head of the serpent/tempter. From this mythic beginning, with the barest outlines of the Covenant of Grace in view, covenant theologians discovered other biblical texts, that described the Covenant of Grace: God preserved faithful Noah and his family, blessed Abraham and Sarah with Isaac, exalted David and Solomon, protected the people Israel, and eventually sent the Messiah—Jesus Christ, the ultimate "seed of the woman"—to conquer sin once for all.

Even this oversimplified sketch of covenant theology should make evident the creative manner in which it attempted to integrate what appeared to be the mutually exclusive claims of divine sovereignty and human responsibility. In the covenant scheme God took the initiative in salvation and accepted full responsibility for the outcome of the covenant. Yet divine sovereignty, far from overwhelming human activity, worked subjectively, in and with individuals as they experienced redemption in Jesus Christ. Although the covenant idiom played an important theological role within the Reformed tradition, however, the social implications of the covenant became increasingly important. In the New World, for instance, the several Puritan "Bible commonwealths" were organized largely on a covenantal basis, wherein citizens viewed themselves individually and corporately as covenant partners with God and with one another.

REDEMPTION IN CHRIST

The quest for the knowledge of God and the knowledge of humanity in Reformed thought finds its primary context in the study of soteriology (from the Greek *soteria*, meaning salvation). The drama of salvation begins with attention to the doctrine of human depravity, moves to a consideration of the work of Christ on behalf of sinners, and then to the legal or moral implications of that redemptive work.

Many Reformed thinkers historically affirmed a federal, or representative interpretation to account for both the origins and transmission of human depravity.[9] Viewing Adam as the divinely ordained representative head of humanity, created in the image of God and morally free to obey or disobey the divine law, Reformed theologians believe that Adam's importance lay in his action on behalf of all his progeny. For good or ill, humanity's destiny was permanently aligned with Adam's. If he conformed to the strictures of the Covenant of Works, then he and his progeny would prosper; if he failed to uphold his covenantal obligations, then humanity would share his punishment. Hence, Adam and Eve's first or original sin not only resulted in their ejection from paradise but also brought about the corruption of the entire human race. God transferred or imputed the guilt of the first sin, committed by humanity's federal representative, to all who were federally related to him. This imputation process, whereby moral qualities were transferred from one person to another, would play equally important roles in other elements of Reformed soteriology, especially the atonement and justification.

Given this analysis of the origins and transmission of evil to humanity at large, it remained for Reformed divines to describe the two-fold effect of depravity on the human soul. There was, first, spiritual and moral depravity that resulted from the imputation of Adam's guilt. This hereditary depravity affected everyone and was diffused throughout the various facets and faculties of each human being—physical, psychological, intellectual, social, spiritual. Because a holy God could not accept anything but perfect moral purity, this hereditary disposition to evil put all people under the wrath and judgment of God. In the strictest schools of Reformed thought, therefore, even infants who appeared incapable of intelligible acts, immoral or otherwise, were identified as sinners. A second effect of depravity followed naturally on the heels of this inherited corruption. Precisely because people were inherently depraved, they sinned as a matter of course: Original sin produced actual sin, further compounding humanity's guilt. The Reformed doctrine of depravity, therefore, can be summarized as follows: all humanity fell in Adam; each person was radically corrupted; everyone sinned voluntarily as a natural consequence of his or her depravity; and all men and women were thus damnable before God.

The corporate aspect of depravity, however, had a complementary correlative in Reformed soteriology. For just as the first Adam had served as the federal head of the entire race, so Christ, the second Adam, acted on behalf of all the elect whom God had chosen to redeem. Offering attestation of his identity through profound teaching and miracle, the incarnate Christ's ultimate sacrifice in the drama of the Covenant of Grace was his atoning death. Once again, Reformed systematists, beginning with strong affirmation of the Bible, adopted concepts and language with which they were already familiar: covenant, federal headship, and the transmission of moral and spiritual qualities from one representative to another person.

Among the first generations of Reformed theologians a loose consensus emerged about many facets of the doctrine of the atonement. Many interpreters agreed that in the atonement Christ took upon himself the consequences of the sins of humanity. In this, the doctrine of imputation was utilized again. Just as Adam's sin had been imputed to humanity, so humanity's sin—be it original or actual—was transferred to Christ. But unanimity among interpreters about such fundamentals was hard to find. Beginning in the late sixteenth and early seventeenth centuries, several critical interpretive questions arose and, around these, several competing doctrines. One important question concerned the extent of the atonement. Most interpreters agreed that Christ's shed blood was of such inestimable value as to make his sacrifice sufficient to save every sinner. By the opening decades of the seventeenth century, however, theologians found themselves divided over the question of the efficiency of the atonement: Was Christ's blood shed for all, or only for the elect? If Christ was, like Adam, a federal head of humanity, did the effects of his perfect obedience to divine law extend to all humanity, as had Adam's disobedience? Was the atonement general in this respect—did Christ die on behalf of all humanity? Or was Christ's sacrificial atonement limited—only intended for the elect?

Those who argued for a limited atonement were able to fit this doctrine rather neatly into their predestination scheme. To their way of thinking, God, before the foundations of the world, decreed that all humanity would fall in Adam and that Christ would redeem the elect. Under this interpretation, Christ died only for the smaller, elect group; to suggest otherwise would be to argue that Christ had shed his blood for people whom God had no intention of redeeming. Some Reformed divines objected to limited atonement, however. These dissenters argued that, although the logic of systematic thinking seemed to undergird the limited atonement, the Bible did not teach it. Despite their objections, however, the limited atonement rapidly became identified as a central element of Reformed orthodoxy.

In Reformed soteriology the notion of imputation also functioned in the doctrine of justification. Like both original sin and the atonement, justification was construed in legal terms. The first imputation (of original sin, from Adam to humanity) was effected by God in the counsels of eternity. The second imputation (of humanity's sin, from the elect to Christ) was initiated by God as a gesture of mercy. But this third imputation (of Christ's righteousness, from Christ to the elect), though initiated by God, was also dependent on the voluntary assent of the individual. Justification was understood to be the gracious act of God in which a sinner was declared righteous on the basis of the imputed righteousness of Christ. Moreover, justification came by grace through faith alone. Utterly incapable of performing righteous acts apart from the immediate influence of the power of God, the sinner attached herself or himself to Christ by faith— itself a divine gift. Lest some might argue that this scheme detracted from a proper emphasis on good works, Reformed thinkers were quick to point out that genuine faith would inevitably produce genuine good works. But faith in Christ and his imputed righteousness is what justified individuals before the eternal judge, not the inherent value of good works themselves.

Although Reformed soteriology was framed by a host of doctrinal idioms— representative headship, covenant theology, divine judgment, imputation, and mercy—this branch of Reformed doctrine also had a distinctly existential character. The sinner was drawn into the legal web, as it were, by the heartstrings. God, in the person of the Holy Spirit, who was particularly active throughout the subjective experience of salvation, regenerated the elect. By means of this intimate process, their hardened hearts were softened. They experienced a new yearning for the knowledge of God and became passionately interested in salvation. At heart, then, Reformed theology was deeply spiritual. Legal language and logical subtlety notwithstanding, the traditional goal of Reformed theology was individual piety.

LIFE IN THE SPIRIT

The doctrines of predestination, the covenant, original sin, justification by the imputation of Christ's righteousness—all of them integral to federal theology— are often viewed as characteristic marks of the Reformed branch of Protestantism. Despite its reputation for intellectually demanding, integrated, and systematic doctrinal systems, however, the Reformed tradition has consistently been as concerned with holy living as it has been with right doctrine. The doctrine of sanctification, like so many other Reformed affirmations, is grounded in a creative tension between divine sovereignty and human responsibility. Reformed theology affirms the sovereignty of the Holy Spirit, but it also insists on the moral duty of Christians to become holy people. The Spirit moves and acts on its own divine initiative, independent of human vice and virtue. Nonetheless, Christians are required to attain some degree of holiness in this life; they are to become like Christ, the perfectly incarnated image of the divine. This tension, however problematic, is framed by the same paradox that attends the whole of Reformed doctrine: As believers strive to know the inscrutable, sovereign God, they come to a deeper, more subtle knowledge of themselves. Knowledge of the divine and self-knowledge, therefore, are intimately connected.

Among Reformed theologians, the notion of progress is central to understanding sanctification; like Christian in *Pilgrim's Progress*, the believer is in the midst of a pilgrimage toward sanctification. Unlike other Protestant attempts to describe how a person becomes holy, notably the Wesleyan or Holiness schemes that became popular in nineteenth-century America, Reformed theologians understand sanctification as a life-long process characterized by rather predictable progress or growth in grace. Whereas Wesleyan theologians argue that the Christian life is characterized by two distinctive steps—conversion and, later, sanctification, in which the Christian suddenly attains new heights of "perfect love" for God—the Reformed theologian reaches back to the older Catholic tradition in which the Christian, over the course of time, exhibits increasing degrees of holiness. Perfection, in the Reformed scheme, lays only in the eschatological future. In heavenly bliss, Christians are glorified with Christ; their spiritual senses and their love for God are refined and purified only then.

One of the chief virtues of the Reformed scheme is that it takes seriously the abiding problem of sin. Although the Christian has been converted to Christian faith under divine initiative, the believer is liable to the effects of sin throughout life. This is not to say that in the Reformed understanding sin can frustrate the work of grace. Indeed, the doctrines of predestination and election serve as a reminder that the elect are eternally secure; they do not fall in and out of grace. Although Christians continue to sin, the moral effects of their former state and the habits that attended it are slowly eradicated over the course of years of life in the Spirit. Reformed Christians exult not in their own accomplishments but in the gracious promise of the sovereign God, in the power of the sanctifying Spirit, and in the assurance of the forgiveness of sins.

THE COMMUNITY OF FAITH

The first three books of Calvin's *Institutes* treat the distinctive roles of the members of the Trinity in the salvation of the people of God. In the fourth and final book, however, Calvin turned to a lengthy examination of the church, or as he preferred, the "Society of Christ." Historically, the sub-traditions within Reformed Protestantism have, at least in general, shared a common affirmation of the basic principles outlined in the first three books of the *Institutes*. That general unanimity, however, has been less evident when it comes to the rubric of ecclesiology, the doctrine of the church. Indeed, the wide diversity of theological reflection about the nature and ministry of the church—debates about polity, authority, church membership, and the sacraments, for instance—has served to divide the larger Reformed tradition into a plethora of constitutent ecclesiastical bodies. Here, under a description of ecclesiology, the central affirmations of the most prominent American branch of Reformed Protestantism, Presbyterianism, begin to emerge.

Calvin and other early reformers worked tirelessly to clarify the fundamental differences between the competing Protestant and Roman Catholic understandings of the nature of the church and its government. This effort led him to identify what he believed were the two distinguishing marks of the church: the true preaching and hearing of the Word of God and the proper administration of the sacraments. By translating the Scriptures into the vernacular, by reemphasizing the preaching ministry, by liberating sacramental theology from what they considered to be the grasping power of the Roman clergy, and by stressing the "priesthood of all believers," Calvin and his co-laborers sought to revitalize the laity and reassert their proper role in the participation of the life of the church.

Unlike the Lutheran *Augsburg Confession* and the later *First Scots Confession*, however, Calvin did not identify church discipline as a characteristic mark of the church. Although he did examine the problem of church purity and outlined procedures whereby a true church might judiciously separate itself from a false church, he never went so far as to identify discipline as a bona fide mark of the Christian Church. Whether this omission was intentional or merely accidental remains a question of some historical importance. In either case, however, it seems prescient, for the issue of proper disciplinary function of the church became a hotly contested matter among later Presbyterians, especially in America.

The Reformed churches conformed, in many respects, to other Protestant ecclesiastical bodies. Like the Lutherans, Anglicans, and the churches of the Radical Reformation, Reformed bodies rejected Roman Catholic soteriology as well as prevailing Roman Catholic models of worship, the sacraments, and the ministry of ordained clergy. The use of Latin was dropped and the liturgy was performed in the vernacular; many of the ornate accouterments that had graced Roman sanctuaries were removed; preaching became a more central feature of the service of worship, often taking prominence over the celebration of the Eucharist. Reformed churches reduced the number of the sacraments from the traditional seven (Baptism, Confirmation, Holy Communion, Penance, Extreme Unction, Marriage, and Holy Orders) to two (Baptism and Holy Communion), and the laity were encouraged to partake of both elements, bread and wine, in Holy Communion. Reformed thinkers also formed a new theology of ordination: They denied that the Bishop of Rome was the preeminent ruler of the church universal, that the clergy must remain celibate, and that monasteries and convents were spiritual gateways to the quickest route to salvation. Beyond these general similarities with other Protestants, however, different ecclesiastical bodies within the larger Reformed tradition developed their own particular understandings of the nature and ministry of the church. At this juncture, therefore, we turn to the two bodies of doctrine that became the distinguishing theological features of Presbyterianism: sacramental theology and ecclesiastical polity.

Reformed theologians believed that a sacrament was a sensible, visible sign that represented a spiritual reality and had been instituted by Christ in the New Testament. Such signs, they argued, had no intrinsic power whatever. Rather, the power and importance of a sacrament lay in its capacity to represent, seal, and apply Christ's benefits to the believer. Like most other Protestants, the Reformed were anxious to distance themselves from the Catholic notion of *ex opere operato*, the dogma that taught that the sacraments, if rightly administered, would transmit divine grace to a properly disposed recipient. Although Reformed theologians contested several substantive points among themselves (e.g., the particular efficacy of the various sacramental elements, the consecrated water, bread, or wine), in general they taught that the sacraments were visible tokens of divine grace and that sacramental grace occurred to the extent that the recipient could appreciate and appropriate the thing symbolized by the sign. Baptism symbolized incorporation into Christ, the descent into death, the ascent to resurrection and new life, the washing away of sin, and the ingrafting of the recipient into the corporate community of faith. Holy Communion (more commonly referred to as the Lord's Supper among Presbyterians) symbolized Christ's broken body and shed blood in the bread and cup.

Among the Reformed Christians who would become Presbyterians, there was general unanimity regarding baptism. This rite of inclusion into the community of faith was properly administered to two categories of people: previously unbaptized, professing adults, and the children of professing church members. In this respect, then, it can be said that Presbyterians affirm both *pedobaptism* (the baptism of young children who are, by virtue of their age, incapable of moral accountability or repentance) and *believer's baptism* (the baptism of repentant adults who seek church membership).

Perhaps the most important distinction to be made concerning Presbyterian pedobaptism has to do with its relationship to the doctrine of original sin. In the traditional Roman Catholic sacramental system, the effect of baptism is twofold; it washes away the effects of original sin and spiritually regenerates the recipient. Although the administration of infant baptism among Presbyterians is similar to the Roman Catholic rite (the child is sprinkled with water in the name of the Father, Son, and Holy Spirit), Presbyterians interpret this event very differently; original sin is not removed by baptism, nor is the child regenerated. Rather, when the sign of washing, or of the descent to death and the ascent of resurrection, is administered, the infant recipient becomes a member of the community of faith. In the Presbyterian tradition, responsibility for the spiritual well-being of the infant falls on the child's parents (who must themselves be church members) and on the other adults who witness the baptism, all of whom vow to rear the baptized child "in the nurture and the admonition of the Lord." For Presbyterians, baptism is a sign of hope, commitment, and inclusion. The community prays that God will spiritually regenerate the child, it promises to do all in its power to witness to the love and salvation of God, and it designates the child a nonconfessing, infant member of the covenant community.

Just as Presbyterians consistently have rejected the Roman Catholic understanding of baptism, so they have also denied the traditional Roman doctrine of the Mass, in which the sacramental elements of bread and wine actually become the body and blood of Christ. In place of the Roman doctrine, Presbyterians affirmed one of several alternative Reformed eucharistic theologies.[10] The first of these stems from Huldrych Zwingli, who, in an attempt to avoid the Reformation debates about the meaning of Jesus' words, "This is my body" and "This is my blood," made Jesus' "Do this in remembrance of me" the operative commandment of the Supper. Sometimes called memorialism, the Zwinglian view holds that the believer, in partaking the symbols of Christ's body and blood, should remember the historic events represented by the symbols, namely the salvific events of Christ's crucifixion. Eschewing the Roman Catholic notion that the elements are transubstantiated into the actual body and blood of Christ in the sacrifice of the Mass and the Lutheran notion that Christ is physically present in the Supper (though the elements are not themselves transubstantiated), the Zwinglian interpretation affirms the strictly symbolic and memorial value of the Supper.

Calvin's understanding of the Lord's Supper, the second major Reformed option, differed substantially from the Roman and Lutheran views, but was also distinct from the Zwinglian interpretation. On the one hand, Calvin and his disciples wanted to avoid Luther's literalistic insistence that Christ's words "This is my body" must be interpreted to mean that Christ was physically present in the Supper. On the other hand, however, Reformed theologians believed that Zwingli's memorialism robbed the Lord's Supper of its capacity to offer recipients spiritual nurture. Hence, taking something of a middle position, the Calvinists affirmed Christ's spiritual (but not physical) presence in the Supper. Although some Presbyterians have leaned toward the Zwinglian position, the majority of Presbyterian bodies affirm the Calvinistic interpretation. Christ is not corporeally present in the elements, nor is the rite merely a remembrance of the grace of God. Rather, Christ is spiritually present in the Eucharist, and the believer, spiritually feeding on the body and blood, receives the benefits of Christ's death and resurrection.

POLITY

The Presbyterian form of ecclesiastical polity has become one of the three classic forms of church government. Unlike both episcopal polity (in which a bishop has the central authority within the body, as in the Roman Catholic, Episcopal, and Methodist traditions) and congregational polity (in which authority is lodged in the local congregation, as in the Congregational and Baptist traditions), presbyterian polity is based on the conviction that the church is properly based on a representative system of government in which ecclesial authority is lodged in a specially elected group of people called the presbytery. The biblical term *presbuteros*, from which Presbyterians derive their name, forms the center of this understanding of ecclesiastical polity.

In the Presbyterian tradition, each local congregation is governed by a body called a *session*. Members of the session are called elders or presbyters and are elected from among members of the local congregation. The needs of the local congregation are also served by a second group of officers known as deacons. Whereas the elders or presbyters traditionally concern themselves with preaching, teaching, worship, and discipline within the local body and at the presbytery level, the deacons minister to the physical needs of the congregation. They attend to the special needs of the poor, the bereaved, and the homeless.

Just as the session is the representative body that governs the local congregation, so the presbytery is the representative body that governs a number of congregations in a particular geographic region. Because the presbytery is charged with the oversight of several local bodies, it attends to a large and varied agenda, including finance, theological training, Christian education, church discipline, and the oversight of ecumenical endeavors. The hierarchical arrangement of representative bodies continues at two levels above the presbytery. The *synod*, made up of representatives from the presbyteries, meets less frequently than the presbytery and, in the American setting, usually represents presbyteries from several states. The only national body of Presbyterianism, located atop the hierarchical structure, is the General Assembly, which meets annually. The Assembly is chaired by a specially elected moderator and conducts its business by means of an often-complex series of standing committees and special task forces.

REFORMED PROTESTANTISM IN EUROPE PRIOR TO THE COLONIZATION OF THE NEW WORLD

Reformed Protestantism had its genesis in the Swiss Reformation under the leadership of Bullinger, Zwingli, Farel, and Calvin, but it quickly spread across Europe and became a powerful religious force in several different cultural contexts. By the mid-seventeenth century Reformed Protestantism was firmly enculturated, albeit in different ways, in Switzerland, France, Germany and Eastern Europe, the Netherlands, and the British Isles. Although it is historically inaccurate to identify the Reformed churches in these nations as strictly Calvinistic or Presbyterian, developments within the larger European Reformed tradition gave definitive shape to the Presbyterian tradition in America.[11]

The political situation had allowed for the rapid growth of Reformed Protestantism in Switzerland during the first generations of the Reformation, but political vicissitudes retarded its growth in France. Seeking to maintain a delicate political alignment with the papacy, the French monarchy had strenuously resisted Protestantism's initial advances. In October 1534, for instance, first-generation Parisian Protestants had, under cover of darkness, distributed a broadside pamphlet against the abuses of the Mass. The Catholic monarch, Francis, quickly retaliated by imprisoning and executing supposed perpetrators. Persecution of Protestants began, rising to a bloody crescendo on the eve of St. Bartholomew's Day in 1572, when some 70,000 French Protestants—known as Huguenots—were slain. Although this massacre was hailed as the decisive end of French Protestantism, the movement, fed by a cadre of ministers trained in Geneva, continued to make inroads among the powerful middle classes. By 1598, with the passage of the Edict of Nantes, Reformed Protestantism was given an official respite from persecution, a privilege the Huguenots enjoyed until its revocation in 1685.

Although Germany is often identified as both the starting place of the Reformation and the stronghold of European Lutheranism, Reformed Protestantism also took root in Germany and parts of Eastern Europe. During the 1550s tensions between Lutherans and the Reformed grew considerably, and to the dismay of many Lutherans, in 1561 Elector Frederick III sponsored efforts by a group of Reformed theologians, including Caspar Olevianus and Zacharias Ursinus, to compose a statement of Reformed faith. Their labors led to the 1563 publication of the most famous European Reformed creed, *The Heidelberg Catechism*. It received nearly universal acceptance among the Reformed throughout Europe, and rapidly became a rival to the Lutheran standard of orthodoxy, *The Augsburg Confession*.

Reformed faith was extraordinarily successful in the Netherlands, where it greatly influenced important cultural institutions—education, the state, and the arts. The most famous meeting of Reformed theologians in the Low Countries took place at the Synod of Dort, held in 1618 and 1619. Jacob Arminius and, after his death in 1609, his Remonstrant school, developed a severe critique of the double predestination scheme developed by Theodore Beza, William Perkins, and others. Over the course of a decade, however, their complaints coalesced into a broader series of interrelated challenges to the reigning orthodoxy. In 1619, the Remonstrant school suffered defeat when the Synod issued a series of five canons that explicitly denounced the "Arminian" position as heresy.[12] These canons, each of which affirmed a central tenet of Calvinist orthodoxy, became popularly known as the "five points of Calvinism."[13]

Although Reformed faith greatly affected cultural developments on the Continent, its history in the British Isles is most pertinent to the story of the American Presbyterian tradition. There is little doubt that the Reformed Protestantism of Geneva greatly influenced the development and outcome of both the Scottish and English Reformations. Chief among the Scottish Reformed divines was John Knox, who became engaged in the cause of reform in 1546. Despite arrest and eighteen months of forced labor on a French galley, he managed to flee to England, where he came under the influence of Archbishop Thomas Cramner. Knox later studied in Geneva with Calvin and returned to Edinburgh after the Elizabethan Settlement in 1559 charted a middle course for the Church of England between Protestantism and Roman Catholicism. Although he was in thorough agreement with English Protestants regarding the central affirmations of Reformed theology, Knox battled for the freedom and independence of the Scottish Church, known as the Kirk. His chief contribution to Presbyterianism lay in his efforts to establish a presbyterian polity distinct from the English episcopacy and to develop Reformed liturgical forms for the Kirk.

The history of the English Reformation is extraordinarily complex for a number of reasons. In the 1530s the reigning monarch of Britain, Henry VIII, led the initial revolt against the hegemony of the Roman Church for largely personal and political reasons. Although his son, Edward VI, reigned briefly as Britain's Protestant child monarch, Henry's daughter Mary Tudor took the throne in 1553 and attempted to return England to the Roman fold. Not until 1559, one year after another of Henry's daughters, Elizabeth I, became queen, was Protestantism finally established in England in a form dictated by the Elizabethan Settlement, a compromise between Protestantism and Catholicism. From the start the Church of England was a complicated blend of liturgy and doctrine. Its official liturgy, *The Book of Common Prayer* (1549), maintained many of the rituals of the Roman tradition, but its official doctrinal summary, *The Thirty-Nine Articles* (1563), was distinctly Reformed in tenor. This composite nature brought a measure of political tranquility, but it also fostered dissent, most notably over the episcopal polity of the Church of England, in which bishops—with the blessing of the queen—wielded ecclesial power and authority. Advocates of the other two forms of ecclesiastical polity, congregationalism and presbyterianism, attempted to build English institutions that would overcome what they considered to be the inherent liabilities of the "popish" episcopal system.

Congregationalism, a polity that would later characterize the Baptist tradition as well as the churches of New England, developed under the English Puritans, who sought to "purify" the Church of England of all vestiges of Roman Catholicism. Fearing the debilitating effects of unregenerates within the membership of the Church, ministers of Puritan sentiment urged their congregations to seek conversion on a distinctly Reformed soteriological model. Some Puritan congregations left the Church of England, although they denied that they had become schismatic separatists.[14]

The ecclesial hegemony of the Church of England also fostered a growth of interest in presbyterian polity. By the 1570s several English theologians became convinced that presbyterian polity was thoroughly biblical. John Field, Walter Tavers, and Thomas Cartwright all appealed to Parliament for reform of the church on a presbyterian model, and all were persecuted for their beliefs. For several decades the history of English Presbyterianism was both intertwined with that of the English Puritans and overshadowed by the Presbyterian successes in Ireland and Scotland.[15]

Notwithstanding these vicissitudes, however, English Presbyterianism left a marvelous legacy to the international Presbyterian tradition—the Westminster Assembly of Divines. Called by Parliament in July 1643, and with the support of the Scottish Kirk and several Reformed divines on the Continent, the Assembly was charged with the full reform of church government and doctrine. Although a complex web of political circumstances prevented the Assembly from fulfilling its optimistic program of reform in England, in six years it produced a series of creedal statements that became authoritative Presbyterian theological standards and, in some quarters, remain so even today: *The Form of Presbyterial Church Government* (1644), *The Directory of Public Worship* (1644), *The Westminster Confession of Faith* (1647), *The Larger Catechism* (1647), and *The Shorter Catechism* (1647).

Although neither Reformed theology nor Presbyterian polity were indigenous to the North American colonies, Presbyterian faith was quickly woven into the fabric of colonial America. European expressions of Reformed Christianity, newly articulated for English-speaking believers in the Westminster standards, provided Presbyterian colonists with helpful reminders of their Protestant heritage. Guided by Westminster, and in the shadow of their Reformed cousins in Puritan New England, Presbyterians in the Middle Colonies set out to establish their particular version of the genuine Christian church. Unlike the American Puritans, however, who hoped to establish new ecclesiastical structures, American Presbyterians had a great deal of experience and wisdom on which to draw. And precisely because their tradition had been enculturated in so many different settings, they successfully laid the foundations for what would become one of America's most durable and dynamic Protestant denominations.

NOTES

1. For a thorough account of the interplay of social and religious themes in the Reformation era, see Steven Ozment, *The Age of Reform, 1250–1550: An Intellectual and Religious History of Late Medieval and Reformation Europe* (New Haven, Conn.: Yale University Press, 1980).

2. The most recent treatment of Zwingli's theology is W. P. Stephens, *The Theology of Huldrych Zwingli* (New York: Oxford University Press, 1986). See also George R. Potter, *Zwingli* (New York: Cambridge University Press, 1976).

3. For a recent treatment of Bullinger's theology and his contributions to the larger Reformed tradition, see J. Wayne Baker, *Heinrich Bullinger and the Covenant: The Other Reformed Tradition* (Athens: Ohio University Press, 1980).

4. Two highly regarded interpretations of Calvin's life are T.H.L. Parker, *John Calvin: A Biography* (Philadelphia: Westminster Press, 1975), and William James Bouwsma, *John Calvin: A Sixteenth-Century Portrait* (New York: Oxford University Press, 1988). For an overview of Calvin's theology, see Francois Wendel, *Calvin: The Origins and Development of His Religious Thought*, trans. Philip Mairet (New York: Harper & Row, 1963).

5. The present volume uses the expressions "Reformed tradition" and "Reformed theology" advisedly. Like any other religious movement, the Reformed tradition is not monolithic. Rather, it has been and continues to be characterized by internal diversity and, at points, contentious disharmony. The reliance on Calvin's *Institutes* in the following pages is justified, we judge, on the basis of its own systematic, comprehensive nature and on its popularity among American Presbyterians. Nonetheless, J. Wayne Baker's caveat in *Heinrich Bullinger and the Covenant*, needs to be taken seriously: "Reformed Protestantism, then, has never been a unitary tradition. Rather, there has been a dual tradition from the beginning. One thrust, initiated by Zwingli, was fully defined and to a-large extent created by Bullinger. The second thrust found its clearest early definition in the thought and church polity of Calvin. Most often this dual tradition has been ignored, and it has never been investigated in any depth" (p. xxiii).

6. The standard scholarly edition of Calvin's *Institutes* is John Calvin, *Institutes of the Christian Religion*, 2 vols., ed. John T. McNeill, The Library of Christian Classics, vol. 20 (Philadelphia: Westminster Press, 1960).

7. For a historical introduction to the Reformed tradition with special emphasis on ecclesial matters, see John H. Leith, *An Introduction to the Reformed Tradition: A Way of Being the Christian Community*, rev. ed. (Atlanta: John Knox Press, 1977).

8. The focus here on the Reformed tradition should not be construed to suggest that other Protestant theologians did not treat the problem of predestination in their work. A

signal example of this is to be found in Martin Luther's classic treatise *The Bondage of the Will*. The standard collection of primary documents illustrating historic Reformed doctrine of the sixteenth and seventeenth centuries is Heinrich Heppe, *Reformed Dogmatics Set Out and Illustrated From the Sources*, trans. G. T. Thomson, ed. Ernest Bizer (London: George & Unwin, 1956). For a recent secondary treatment of the predestination problem, see Richard A. Muller, *Christ and the Decree: Christology and Predestination in Reformed Theology From Calvin to Perkins* (Durham, N.C.: Labyrinth Press, 1986).

9. For a recent pathbreaking account of the origins of this federal system, see David A. Weir, *The Origins of Federal Theology in Sixteenth-Century Reformation Thought* (New York: Oxford University Press, 1990).

10. For a useful treatment of the various views of the Lord's Supper among Reformed theologians, see Brian A. Gerrish, "Sign and Reality: The Lord's Supper in the Reformed Confessions," in Brian A. Gerrish, *The Old Protestantism and the New: Essays on the Reformed Heritage* (Chicago: University of Chicago Press, 1982), pp. 118–130.

11. John T. McNeill, *The History and Character of Calvinism* (New York: Oxford University Press, 1954) remains an outstanding account of the development of Calvinism in Europe and the New World. For a series of essays on the diversity and geographic spread of Reformed thought into particular regions see *John Calvin: His Influence in the Western World*, ed. W. Stanford Reid (Grand Rapids, Mich.: Zondervan, 1982).

12. Use of the term "Arminian" has a rather dubious history. Most properly, Arminian theology refers to that body of thought promulgated by Arminius and the Remonstrants at Dort. The term is used in at least two other contexts, however. Often, in a partisan manner, it describes any doctrine or person that is forthrightly anti-Calvinist. For instance, John Wesley, the founder of Methodism, is often referred to (rather mistakenly) as an "Arminian" because of his reservations about the Reformed doctrine of double predestination. This semantic problem is further exacerbated, however. Some eighteenth-century Anglo-American Enlightenment thinkers—ranging from Deists to skeptical "rationalists"—bear the appellation "Arminian" due to their rejection of traditional Calvinism's severe doctrine of human depravity. In fact, this latter group had little in common with classic Arminianism, which, notwithstanding its rejection of several tenets of orthodox Calvinism, affirmed a broad range of traditional Christian doctrines.

13. References to the "five points of Calvinism" are often misleading. Calvinist theology is complex and carefully nuanced, and is not readily or accurately reduced to a simple list of affirmations. Scholars continue to debate questions surrounding the direct influence of Calvin's theology on the subsequent Reformed tradition and on the roles played by Beza and Perkins in the development of "Calvinism." For a particularly pointed analysis of this historical problem see R. T. Kendall, *Calvin and English Calvinism to 1649* (New York: Oxford University Press, 1979); Paul Helm, *Calvin and the Calvinists* (Edinburg and Carlisle, Pa.: Banner of Truth, 1982); and the entire issue of the *Evangelical Quarterly* 55:2 (1983).

14. The secondary literature treating Puritanism is extraordinarily complex and rich. Perry Miller, *The New England Mind: The Seventeenth Century* (New York: Macmillan, 1939) remains one of the best overall treatments of the movement. David D. Hall, "Understanding the Puritans," reprinted in *Religion in American History: Interpretive Essays*, ed. John M. Mulder and John F. Wilson (Englewood Cliffs, N.J.: Prentice-Hall, 1977), is a useful analysis of the problem of defining the term *Puritan*. Charles L. Cohen,

God's Caress: The Psychology of Puritan Religious Experience (New York: Oxford University Press, 1986), provides an excellent description of Puritan spirituality.

15. For a sustained historical account of the relationship between Puritans and Presbyterians in England, see Patrick Collinson, *The Elizabethan Puritan Movement* (Berkeley and Los Angeles: University of California Press, 1967).

2
THE COLONIAL ERA

The adventure of the Pilgrims and the Puritans in founding New England has long captured the imagination of Americans—choosing to leave the Old World, making the long and perilous voyage, encountering native Americans in an alien land, carving a society out of the wilderness. Although some of the Puritans who migrated across the Atlantic also had presbyterian sympathies, the earliest Puritan settlers could not, in truth, be called Presbyterians. The settlement of Presbyterians in the New World is a good deal less prosaic and, hence, less familiar.

By the time James VI of Scotland ascended the English throne (thereby becoming James I of the United Kingdom), a series of unsuccessful conspiracies in northern Ireland had led to the forfeiture of large territories to the crown. This windfall, in turn, opened the way for the "great plantation" of the province of Ulster by English and Scottish colonists. The prospect of a new land and fresh opportunities held considerable allure for Scots, especially for Lowlanders mired in poverty, and from 1610 through the end of the century Lowland Scots migrated to northern Ireland in large numbers. Further confiscation of Irish lands by Oliver Cromwell after the Rebellion of 1641 and by William of Orange after the Glorious Revolution of 1688 increased the territory available for colonization.

The migration of Scots to Ulster reached its zenith between the years 1690 and 1697. The Scots carried with them to Ireland skills in farming, trade, and manufacturing. The majority also brought a stout allegiance to Presbyterianism. Two Stuart kings, Charles I and II, tried coercing these immigrants into renouncing Presbyterianism and embracing the Church of England (whereby, presumably, they would become better subjects) but the activities of Scottish Presbyterian ministers among the Ulster Scots together with persistent religious and ethnic loyalties turned back those threats.

Economic stringency—rack-renting, famine, the decline of the linen industry, and repressive trade laws, particularly the restrictions on woolen exports—

prompted many Scots-Irish to migrate to America late in the seventeenth century and early in the eighteenth. The Scots-Irish also had other reasons for seeking a new land: the lack of strong loyalties to Ireland and religious repression at the hands of the established Church of Ireland. The Test Act of 1704 forbade all dissenters, including Ulster Presbyterians, from holding civil or military offices by insisting that all who served in those capacities take communion from the established church.

Most of the Scots-Irish Presbyterians who headed for the New World in search of economic opportunity and religious surcease settled in the Middle Colonies, a region marked by religious and ethnic pluralism utterly without parallel on either side of the Atlantic. This area, especially New Jersey and Pennsylvania, became the nexus of colonial Presbyterianism. Scottish immigrants had been coming to America since the 1640s, albeit in small numbers. As the seventeenth century wore on, a few Presbyterians from New England headed south, where, joined by the Scots-Irish, their numbers soon were large enough to justify an appeal to Northern Ireland for ministers.

Francis Makemie,* among several others, answered that call. After his arrival in the New World in 1683, Makemie launched his American career in Maryland, but his itinerancy and his organizational efforts were significant enough to earn him the sobriquet "father of American Presbyterianism." Makemie and other early Presbyterian leaders worked with both the New England strain of Presbyterianism, with its emphasis on experiential—or, in the argot of the day, "experimental"—piety, and with the more confessional faith of Scots-Irish Presbyterians. By the opening of the eighteenth century, Presbyterian churches had been organized in Newark (1667), Elizabeth (1668), Woodbridge (1680), Fairfield (1692), Philadelphia (1692), and several other settlements. American Presbyterianism had matured to the point that some sort of governing structure was necessary.

In accordance with presbyterian polity, Makemie and seven other ministers formed the first American presbytery in 1706, which promptly named Makemie as moderator. The purpose of the new presbytery, in Makemie's words, was "to meet yearly, and oftener if necessary, to consult the most proper measures for advancing religion and propagating religion in our various stations, and to maintain such a correspondence as many conduce to the improvement of our ministerial abilities."[1] A survey of the presbytery's charter members illustrates the various traditions and backgrounds that colonial Presbyterianism drew upon. Samuel Davis, a merchant and pastor at Lewes on the Delaware, had migrated from Ireland. George McNish, a Scot, and John Hampton, a Scots-Irishman, had originally been sent to the colonies by the United Brethren, better known as the Moravians. Three of the founding members came from New England: Nathaniel Taylor, pastor at Patuxent, Maryland; Jedediah Andrews of Philadelphia, the son of New England Presbyterians and a graduate of Harvard College; and John Wilson of New Castle, on the Delaware River. Makemie himself illustrates this melding of traditions better than anyone else. A Scots-Irishman,

*See Preface, p. xi, for explanation.

Makemie had been educated in Scotland, and he maintained strong ties with both England and New England.[2] The leaders of this first American presbytery judiciously avoided thorny theological issues that might have been divisive; their chief objective was unity and the extension of the presbyterian witness, not doctrinal precisionism.

Fed by the continued influx of immigrants, American Presbyterianism grew sufficiently to support seventeen ministers by 1716 and to establish a synod that same year. The General Synod consisted of the Presbytery of Long Island (churches in New York and New Jersey), the Presbytery of Philadelphia (churches in Pennsylvania), the Presbytery of New Castle (churches in the lower Delaware region), and the Presbytery of Snow Hill, which was to have consisted of the churches in Maryland, but which never came into being.

THE ADOPTING ACT OF 1729

Early in the eighteenth century a rift developed among American Presbyterians that roughly paralleled the differences between the New England and the Scots-Irish strains of Presbyterianism. By 1729, the coalition of competing ideologies that Makemie and other founders had fashioned stood in danger of being torn asunder. Would American Presbyterianism define itself according to a bare intellectual assent to dogmatic and creedal definitions as set forth in the Westminster documents? Or would Presbyterians rely more on religious piety, the spiritual and ethical dimensions of the religious life?

A controversy surrounding the issue of the subscription system had engulfed British Presbyterianism for some time. Under this system individuals were required to affirm a particular theological creed. The Solemn League and Covenant of Scotland had demanded subscription to the Westminster standards, and the Revolution Settlement of 1690, which provided legal establishment for Presbyterianism in Scotland, allowed the Church of Scotland to require subscription to the Westminster Confession of Faith as a test of ministerial communion. Similar subscription controversies had raged in England and Ireland.

In America, the issue of subscription arose initially as a reaction to what some Presbyterians regarded as the synod's leniency in dealing with the moral failings of Robert Cross, a young Scots-Irish pastor of the New Castle Presbytery. Although Cross and other emigre ministers were eager to serve, some established ministers questioned the newcomers' credentials. On the floor of the Synod of Philadelphia in 1721, George Gillespie, a minister of New Castle Presbytery, opened a volley of exchanges when he introduced measures that would move American Presbyterianism in the general direction of stricter discipline in the clerical ranks and require subscription to the Westminster standards. The following year Jonathan Dickinson,* Presbyterian from New England, warned against the adoption of strict creedal formulas as a reversion to Romanism and Anglicanism and a betrayal of the sufficiency of the Bible as the guide for faith and life. In 1727, John Thomson, of the New Castle Presbytery, introduced measures explicitly calling upon the synod to demand subscription from every minister and all candidates for the ministry. Dickinson again responded, arguing that such a demand must logically extend to every member of the church, since it was incumbent upon every Christian to defend the gospel. Such a requirement, Dickinson said, would cause confusion and division and would effectively elevate a document crafted by humans (the *Westminster Confession of Faith*) to the level of the Scriptures themselves. The issue thus joined, clerical combatants lined up on one side or the other, with the New England Presbyterians generally supporting Dickinson's less rigorous position and the preponderance of the Scots-Irish favoring subscription.

By the time the synod was gaveled to order in 1729 to resolve the issue, both sides had sharpened their arguments in an exchange of pamphlets. Thomson contended that, in the absence of any superior ecclesiastical body, the synod had to assume responsibility for ensuring the probity and the doctrinal orthodoxy of its ministers and ministerial candidates. It was not sufficient, he said, simply for American Presbyterians to adhere to the Westminster standards by common consent—that could easily lead to dissembling and equivocation. Rather, Thomson insisted that the synod must officially adopt the standards and demand unqualified subscription of its clergy. For Thomson, the theological content of the creed, though not its form, rivaled the authority of Scripture itself.

Dickinson, on the other hand, maintained that "a joint acknowledgment of our Lord Jesus Christ for our common head" and an affirmation of "the sacred Scriptures for our common standard both in faith and practice" together with agreement on worship and discipline was "a sufficient bond of union for the being or well-being of any church under heaven."[3] Dickinson allowed that the Westminster documents had been crafted by honest, godly, faithful men, but he reminded his readers that they were nevertheless a human interpretation of the Scriptures and not the Scriptures themselves. Dickinson conceded that he did not fully understand the Bible, implying that the Westminster divines could not have fully understood it, either, and he suggested that a safer course in the midst of the subscription controversy would be to examine more carefully a candidate's religious experience rather than scrutinizing his beliefs. Finally, he reminded American Presbyterians of the schisms that the subscription controversies had created in Britain.

At the heart of this dispute lay two very different notions of orthodoxy. The subscriptionists, dominated by the Scots-Irish, believed that creedal affirmation would ensure the perpetuation of correct theology. Dickinson and his party, on the other hand, dominated by Presbyterians from England and New England, thought of creeds as mere interpretations of Scripture, subject both to human fallibility and cultural influences. The believer's life, Dickinson said, consisted of more than doctrinal precisionism; indeed, a reliance on creedal affirmation would lead not only to a devaluation of the Bible as the guide to faith and practice but also to a rationalistic faith rather than a warm-hearted piety.

In the end, compromise prevailed over ideology and partisanship.[4] The Adopting Act of 1729, crafted primarily by Dickinson, distinguished between the essential and nonessential components of the Westminster standards. Any minister or ministerial candidate who had reservations about the Westminster articles was required to state his scruples at the time of his subscription. The presbytery would then judge whether or not the scruple could be resolved within the broader outlines of Westminster theology. The synod began applying the criteria almost immediately, inviting anyone with reservations to state them. No one presented an insuperable objection to the Westminster standards, and although the strict subscriptionists were not mollified by the Adopting Act, Dickinson's compromise held American Presbyterianism together for several years, until the Great Awakening rekindled old disputes, albeit in somewhat different guises.

THE GREAT AWAKENING

William Tennent, Sr.,* was one of the first Presbyterians in America to recognize the need for both learning and warm-hearted piety in the clergy. After several years as a pastor in Bedford, New York, he moved to Neshaminy, Pennsylvania, in 1727, and there, in his home, he began preparing a small group of clerical candidates, including his three sons, for the ministry. The growth of Presbyterianism in America, and especially its expansion into sparsely settled frontier areas, had created a demand for pastors that far exceeded the supply of British-educated clergy from across the Atlantic.

The senior Tennent's academy came to be known as the Log College, originally a term of derision. Of the early students, Gilbert Tennent* quickly emerged as the most energetic and insistent preacher, a characteristic that he developed with alacrity during his pastorate in New Brunswick, New Jersey, from 1726 until 1744. At New Brunswick, Tennent fell under the influence of Theodorus Jacobus Frelinghuysen and became enamored of the Dutch pietism that had flourished among the Jersey Dutch since the 1690s. Frelinghuysen, himself a product of Reformed pietism in the Old World, had come to the Raritan Valley in 1720, and his itinerancy in New Jersey had both awakened many souls to the delights of "experimental" piety and engendered considerable acrimony in his churches. Frelinghuysen had insisted that prospective communicants demonstrate some outward sign of regeneration, and his ecclesiastical opponents charged him with favoritism and vindictiveness in applying those tests.

Under Frelinghuysen's influence, Tennent became convinced of his own spiritual apathy (even though he had testified to a conversion experience in his late teens), and he resolved to exercise "greater earnestness in ministerial labours."[5] For Tennent, that meant rousing his congregations from their religious complacency. Mere affirmation of belief in orthodox doctrine or even in the Bible itself was no longer sufficient, he preached. Tennent demanded instead an *experience* of God brought about by a spiritual conversion that included three stages: conviction of sin under the divine law; an experience of spiritual rebirth; and a reformed life that gave evidence of the work of the spirit in practical piety. He repeated this demand countless times in emotional preaching as he itinerated throughout the Middle Colonies and undertook an ambitious program of home visitations. To the unconverted and self-righteous he preached the terrors of the law; to those under conviction, he preached grace and mercy; to the converted, he offered admonitions to piety and godly living. By the close of the 1720s Tennent's congregations, like Frelinghuysen's, were convulsed with religious revival. Gilbert's brother John witnessed a considerable awakening among his congregation at Freehold, New Jersey, a work continued after his death in 1732 by still another brother, William, Jr.

Soon, however, and predictably enough, the revival's success among the Presbyterians engendered a reaction from those suspicious of all the enthusiasm that attended these awakenings. The opponents of the revival charged that the evangelicals were destroying the foundations of orthodoxy by belittling rational religion and emphasizing the religious affections. The synod, meeting at Philadelphia in 1733, passed a general resolution endorsing ''some proper means to revive the declining power of godliness,'' but the measure met with tepid response and even fainter compliance. The next year the subscriptionists, now cast as the antirevivalist party, entered the fray, demanding that the synod check the books of each presbytery to see whether or not subscription was being enforced rigorously. Gilbert Tennent and other evangelicals, in turn, pointed out that the Westminster standards that the antirevivalists were so eager to see enforced included demands that candidates for the ministry demonstrate not only theological proficiency but also evidence of personal piety.

Although Tennent and his brothers had subscribed to the Westminster standards without qualification, his position closely resembled the argument that Dickinson had advanced amidst the subscription controversy of 1729, namely, that Presbyterians pay attention to the spirituality demonstrated by the clergy and not merely to their stated beliefs. Accordingly, the synod in 1734 required that great care be exercised in admitting ministerial candidates and that all ministers be ordered to perform their pastoral duties with all diligence and faithfulness. A heresy trial two years later illustrated the futility of subscription as a means of guaranteeing fidelity to Presbyterian standards. Samuel Hemphill of Philadelphia, tried and convicted of heresy, had twice subscribed to the Westminster standards, once in Ireland and again in America.

While such battles over Presbyterian policy were being waged annually in the synod, Gilbert Tennent and other graduates of his father's Log College continued their work on behalf of the revival. Whatever the success or failure of the evangelicals' initiatives in the councils of the synod, they were making remarkable headway in the field. The Presbyterians' success in the Middle Colonies, together with the revival of piety among the Dutch, matched and even exceeded the religious fervor that Jonathan Edwards was witnessing in Northampton, Massachusetts. The Great Awakening was gathering force.

But the opposition gained momentum nearly as fast. For some reason—because of their itinerancy or because they anticipated controversy—those Presbyterians who supported the Awakening stayed away from the 1736 synod. At that meeting the subscriptionist–antirevival coalition effectively rescinded the Adopting Act of 1729 and, over token opposition, imposed strict, unqualified subscription onto all members of the synod. That action, however, together with subsequent attempts to restrict the movement of the revivalists, galvanized the revival faction—now derisively called "New Lights" by their opponents—into a cohesive party.

At the 1738 synod, the New Lights, headed by Gilbert Tennent, won approval for the establishment of a new presbytery, called the New Brunswick Presbytery, with a large territory extending from Cape May to the Delaware Water Gap. More important, because Presbyterian polity authorized individual presbyteries to train, license, and ordain clergy, the New Lights could perpetuate the revival without struggling against the "Old Light" traditionalists who dominated the Philadelphia Presbytery. The antirevival party, however, struck back, passing a measure in the synod stipulating that any ministerial candidate who did not have a degree from a New England or European college must first sustain an examination administered by a commission of the synod before he could be ordained by a presbytery. This proposal, of course, was directed at Log College graduates who could not produce a college degree, although they were certainly among the most vigorous and effective of the colonial ministers. The New Brunswick presbytery, predictably, refused to comply with the synod's ruling on the grounds that the measure violated Presbyterian polity, which vested the powers of examination and ordination in the presbytery. They offered instead to allow two members of the synod to sit in on their ordination examinations, but the antirevivalists insisted on sending enough representatives to constitute a majority.

The arrival of George Whitefield, the Anglican itinerant, both convulsed the Middle Colonies in revival and hardened Presbyterian rivalries. Whitefield preached to large crowds in Philadelphia on 2 November 1739, and soon, buoyed by his success there and encouraged by the efforts of Log College graduates, Whitefield visited various Presbyterian congregations in the area, preaching his message of moral reform, spiritual renewal, and, often, the need for a regenerated clergy. Such a message did not sit well with the opponents of the revival, but in fact Whitefield's stunning successes, not unlike the publication of Jonathan Edwards's *Faithful Narrative of a Surprising Work of God* in 1737 in New England, roused the faithful in the Middle Colonies and turned the tide against the revival's opponents.

Thus invigorated by Whitefield's example, Presbyterian revivalists preached with redoubled fervor, calling their congregations to repentance and castigating the Old Lights for their opposition to what was undeniably, from the New Light perspective, a work of God. Gilbert Tennent, once again, led the charge. Tennent's most famous sermon was delivered at Nottingham, Pennsylvania, on 8 March 1740. In that sermon, later published and widely circulated as *The Danger of an Unconverted Ministry*, Tennent argued passionately that the opponents of revival were unregenerate themselves and had no divine call to the ministry. These pastors may technically be orthodox in theology, he said, but they were spiritually dead, and, what was worse, they were leading their congregations astray. Mixing law and grace into a jumble of theological confusion, these unconverted ministers failed to lead their auditors from self-righteousness to conviction and on to conversion. Tennent implored his auditors to seek a converted minister through the prescribed channels of Presbyterian polity because, he said, "Success by unconverted Ministers Preaching is very improbable, and very seldom happens, so far as we can gather."[6]

Tennent's sentiments won praise from Log College men as well as from Jonathan Dickinson and the New York Presbytery. In the midst of all his rhetoric about conversion and revival, Tennent also asserted, in the face of resistance from Old Light Presbyterians, that the prerogative for ordination lay with the local presbyteries rather than with the synod. Since 1737, moreover, antirevivalists in the synod had sought to restrict itinerancy as a means of checking the spread of the revival.

The revival's opponents resorted once again to subscription in an attempt to thwart the influence of the New Lights. In 1741 John Thomson proposed shoring up the powers of presbytery and synod by requiring all communicants both to acknowledge those authorities and to subscribe to the Westminster standards. At the meeting of the Synod of Philadelphia that same year, Robert Cross produced a document called the *Protestation*, which declared the New Brunswick revivalists to have forfeited their membership in synod by asserting their powers of ordination. The *Protestation* demanded that the revivalists abjure those powers as a condition for reinstatement into the synod. A majority of the synod hastily signed the *Protestation* on 1 June 1741, thereby, in their words, expelling "some of our members from our communion, on account of irregularity and misconduct in the following of Rev. George Whitefield, one of the English Methodists."[7]

OLD SIDE AND NEW SIDE

The New Lights, thus forced from the synod, were confronted with the task of organizing their churches while simultaneously encouraging the perpetuation of revival fervor and sustaining various missionary efforts on the frontier. After their ejection, they took the name "Conjunct Presbyteries of New Brunswick and Londonderry," while their antirevivalist opponents, led by Scots-Irish subscriptionists, christened themselves the Synod of Philadelphia. Popularly, however, the members of the Synod of Philadelphia were known as Old Side Presbyterians, and members of the revival party as the New Side Presbyterians. After being rebuffed by the Old Side while trying to mediate a rapproachement between the two factions, Jonathan Dickinson and his New York Presbytery withdrew from the Synod of Philadelphia and eventually joined with the revivalists of the New Brunswick Presbytery to form the Synod of New York in 1745.

The new body adhered to the Adopting Act of 1729 and insisted that ministers "have a competent degree of ministerial knowledge, are orthodox in their doctrine, regular in their lives," and diligent in "designs of vital godliness."[8] The

Synod of New York, however, did not stipulate any educational requirements of ministerial candidates that might exclude Log College graduates. Indeed, the new synod explicitly endorsed the revival as a work of God, even as it made overtures toward reunion with the Old Side Synod of Philadelphia.

Having thus wed orthodox doctrine and vital piety, the Synod of New York sought institutional means to perpetuate this elusive pairing. Despite the Old Side–New Side squabbles, American Presbyterianism was entering a period of rapid growth. In 1740 Presbyterians had established approximately ninety-five Presbyterian congregations in the colonies; by 1780, however, that number would grow to nearly five hundred.[9] This rapid congregational growth created a demand for trained clergy, and given the Presbyterian tradition of requiring ministers to have received a formal, classical education, the need for educational institutions among both New Side and Old Side Presbyterians increased.

Several years before his death in 1746, William Tennent, Sr., closed his Log College in Neshaminy. Harvard and Yale were in the hands of those who opposed the revival, so the New Side Presbyterians sought to establish their own school for the training of ministers. Although the number of Presbyterian educational institutions throughout the nation would undergo remarkable growth during the nineteenth century, the College of New Jersey—from which both Princeton University and Princeton Theological Seminary would later develop—became the single most important center of Presbyterian theological education during the eighteenth and much of the nineteenth century.

On 22 October 1746 John Hamilton, interim governor of New Jersey, signed a charter for the College of New Jersey. Largely due to the efforts of New Side partisan Jonathan Dickinson, classes were begun in 1747 in Elizabethtown, New Jersey. Dickinson became the college's first president, but died shortly after the institution began. Fortunately, Governor Jonathan Belcher took up the cause of the college; in its early years he became the fledgling institution's most important friend, guiding the college through the maze of colonial factionalism and metropolitan politics.[10] On Dickinson's death, the board of trustees elected Aaron Burr* to the office of president. During Burr's ten years in office, he moved the college to Princeton, supervised the construction of Nassau Hall—at the time of its completion the grandest college building in the colonies—and put the school on a sound financial footing.

Throughout this period New Side Presbyterians continued their cooperation with other revivalists, especially the Dutch in the Middle Colonies and the Congregational New Lights in New England. This movement culminated in 1758 when the trustees of the College of New Jersey persuaded Jonathan Edwards, perhaps the most celebrated of New England's Congregationalist New Lights, to assume the presidency of the Presbyterian school. But a tragic death once again cast a pall of uncertainty over the school; within weeks of his arrival in Princeton, Edwards died from the complications of a smallpox inoculation.

Within months of Edwards' demise, however, New Side and Old Side Presbyterians negotiated an ecclesiastical treaty and reunited. Despite the Old Side

Synod of Philadelphia's languor and its dim prospects—the number of Old Side clergy decreased from twenty-seven to twenty-three during the schism, while New Side ministers increased to seventy-three from twenty-two—it was the New Side that had made overtures for reconciliation throughout the years of separation, 1741 to 1758. Finally in 1758, after a long sequence of negotiations, the two synods agreed to meet simultaneously in Philadelphia, where on 29 May 1758, following several conciliatory sermons, both sides adopted the Plan of Union hammered out by representatives of the two parties. Thus was born the Synod of New York and Philadelphia. The compromise settlement endorsed the Awakening as a work of God, while acknowledging revival excesses; it allowed some latitude in the acceptance of the Westminster standards; and it affirmed that the powers of ordination lay with the presbyteries.

Vestigial loyalties and suspicions continued to plague American Presbyterianism in the years following the reunion of 1758. Erstwhile Old Side men still preferred doctrinal affirmations as the criteria by which ministers should be judged, while the New Side party looked for evidence of warm-hearted, experimental religion; the Old Side still believed that the fount of Presbyterian orthodoxy lay across the Atlantic, whereas the New Side held that American Presbyterianism possessed a genius all its own, a mixture of ethnic groups leavened by Awakening piety and energized by missionary zeal. Although the 1758 reunion held the disparate strands of American Presbyterianism together for more than half a century, residual animosities between the factions became evident as they struggled to place their respective theological imprimaturs on educational institutions.

In an effort to put the college at Princeton on a sound theological base, New Side strategists had reached beyond denominational barriers—to the Congregationalist Edwards—for leadership. Old Side educators, on the other hand, remained insular, and their designs for expansion into frontier areas were frustrated both by their failure to recruit and train clergy and by the existing clergy's persistent moral failings. In late November 1743, Francis Alison* had addressed the former problem by establishing a school, New London Academy, at New London, Pennsylvania, which won official backing from the Synod of Philadelphia the following year. In contrast to the College of New Jersey, however, the Old Side school foundered for lack of funds and students. After nine years at the helm, Alison left to accept a position at the College of Philadelphia, whereupon the Old Side academy moved to Newark, Delaware, where it was known in successive incarnations as Newark Academy, Newark College, and Delaware College.[11] Alison tried to establish ties between the College of Philadelphia and the Synod of Philadelphia, but that scheme also met with a tepid response.

After the 1758 reunion, New Side partisans continued their efforts to protect their interests in Princeton. New Light firebrand Samuel Davies,* whose pastoral work had helped to establish the Hanover Presbytery in Virginia, Presbyterianism's first foothold in the American South, became the college's fourth president. Like Edwards, Davies's tenure was cut short by his untimely death in 1761, at age thirty-eight. New Side friends of the College next turned to Samuel Finley, one of the early students at the Log College. But again their plans were foiled by death; Finley, the college's fifth president in twenty years, died in 1766.

Finley's death created, once again, a power vacuum in the college administration. As the Board of Trustees scrambled to find and install yet another president who would be acceptable to the college's New Side constituency, recalcitrant Old Siders—despite the ostensible "treaty" of 1758—attempted to wrest control of the college. Their plan, the details of which survive in a letter of Samuel Purviance to Yale's "Gentle Puritan" Ezra Stiles, called for the total reorganization of the college; Francis Alison, stalwart Old Sider, was to become president under the terms of the plan. Success of the Old Side plan largely depended on surprise, but despite attempts at secrecy, details of the planned coup became known. Forewarned, the board met on 19 November 1766 and chose John Witherspoon* of Scotland as their candidate for the presidency.[12] Witherspoon declined the board's first offer to become the college's sixth president. Forced to act before the Old Side could organize another hostile takeover, the board successfully elected Samuel Blair to the presidency. Like many of his predecessors, Blair's presidency was unusually short, although his tenure did not end with his death. At the behest of the board, Benjamin Rush, a Princeton graduate, visited Scotland and urged Witherspoon to reconsider the board's offer. Within two months, word reached the college that Rush's mission had been successful; Witherspoon had agreed to take charge of the college, and Samuel Blair dutifully yielded control of the school to his Scottish successor.

These political machinations notwithstanding, soon after his arrival in Princeton in 1768 Witherspoon became a moderating force between Presbyterianism's factions. His Scottish Presbyterian background and his comprehensive knowledge of continental Reformed theology (both of which were Old Side shibboleths, and both of which would become highly valued theological benchmarks among subsequent generations of Princetonians) plus his reputation for warm-hearted piety (the chief concern among New Side partisans) uniquely qualified Witherspoon to mitigate remaining Old Side–New Side animosities and to recast colonial Presbyterianism along traditional lines. Witherspoon's conciliatory role in the internecine squabbles among America's contentious colonials would in itself earn him a place in American history textbooks, but his efforts on two other fronts also established him as one of American Presbyterianism's most important leaders. The first of Witherspoon's extracurricular labors was largely cultural. Given his Scottish roots, he willingly represented thousands of Scots-Irish Presbyterians who had recently emigrated to the colonies. These Americans, accustomed to the more traditional Presbyterianism of the kirk, rapidly became the dominant ethnic force in American Presbyterianism. Hence, with his election to the presidency of the college, Witherspoon became the most prominent Presbyterian educator in the nation, as well as the titular head of Presbyterianism's most powerful constituency. The second additional field in which Witherspoon left his mark was political. By the mid–1770s, Witherspoon was one of the most prominent clerical apologists for American independence, and he eventually became the only clergyman to sign the Declaration of Independence.

PRESBYTERIANS AND THE AMERICAN REVOLUTION

American Presbyterians, not unlike other colonists, found themselves divided on the most pressing political issues of the 1760s and 1770s. Some conservatives found the very idea of political independence from Britain—despite the legacy of animosity that existed between the Church of England and Presbyterianism— extremely repugnant. By the time the colonies declared their independence from Britain and proved willing to engage the British in armed conflict, however, the ranks of Presbyterian loyalists withered appreciably. The bulk of Presbyterian political sentiment was thus divided into two competing ideologies, the conservative and the radical.

The conservative party in the debates leading up to independence were of two minds about the notion of a political break with England. With many of their fellow colonials, they objected to what they considered to be Britain's improper usurpation of the colonists' political and civil rights. But these moderates, many of whom were upper-class merchants in the established seaboard areas of the colonies, also feared the disastrous consequences of colonial attempts to withdraw from the safety of the Empire. Because they believed that the colonies' interests would be best served in a situation of relative autonomy, these conservative pragmatists attempted to quash intemperate patriotic rhetoric and to negotiate a policy that would appease the demands of both the Crown and the colonies. The radicals of the era, whose ranks swelled during the decade prior to the outbreak of the Revolution, increasingly grew impatient with the ameliorating rhetoric of the conservatives. Made up of "middle sort" frontier folk and working-class urban laborers, the radicals used the revolutionary crisis to voice two sets of grievances—one directed at British political tyranny, the other at the upper, "ruling" class of colonial society.[13] Several Presbyterians—laypeople such as William Livingston* and Abraham Clark and ministers such as Jacob Green and Alexander McWhorter—became leaders of the radical patriot group. But the most prominent among the Presbyterian radicals, particularly in New Jersey, was John Witherspoon. Given his sterling reputation among many Scots-Irish Presbyterians and his powerful position as president of the College of New Jersey, Witherspoon exerted extraordinary influence on behalf of American independence.

By the time that Witherspoon had arrived in Princeton to take up his duties in 1768, the revolutionary spirit had already infused both the college and the town. Students regularly engaged in heated classroom debates on political theory and heard numerous harangues on the duties of true patriotism. At the college commencement of 1765, graduating seniors joined in the nearly universal colonial resistance to the Stamp Act. Eschewing fine clothing, much of which was made with fabric imported from England, they received their degrees dressed in home-spun of colonial manufacture, a modest form of rebellion that would later be repeated at the college and at the commencements of other colonial colleges. The decade of the 1770s, however, brought more pointed displays of American patriotism to the college. In 1770, a public hangman, hired by students for the occasion, burned a copy of the Non-Importation Agreement before the student body and within earshot of the bell atop Nassau Hall, which was rung to solemnize the occasion. In January 1774, just one month after the infamous Boston Tea Party, students burned the college's supply of tea, and with it an effigy of the unpopular Thomas Hutchinson, governor of Massachusetts.[14]

To the dismay of conservatives and loyalists alike (many of whom had hoped that the college president, a native Scot and recent emigre, would avoid entanglement in colonial politics) Witherspoon did nothing to check the college's young Presbyterian "Sons of Liberty." Witherspoon's failure to discipline his young charges was not born of indifference; rather, the students and the political cause they espoused had captured Witherspoon's allegiance, and he happily allowed, even encouraged, the college to become a "hotbed of radical sentiment."[15] Throughout 1775 and 1776 Witherspoon became increasingly involved in politics, first in New Jersey and later at the national level. In sermons, essays, satirical broadsides, and in a large correspondence with other radicals, Witherspoon lent his considerable intellect to the defense of the patriot cause. Seeing an inherent link between religious and civil freedoms, he observed, "There is not a single instance in history in which civil liberty was lost and religious liberty preserved entirely. If therefore we yield up our temporal property, we at the same time deliver the conscience into bondage."[16] In the spring of 1776, Witherspoon became involved in the ouster of New Jersey Governor William Franklin (who, unlike Governor Belcher, had attempted to bring the college under governmental control) and in the forming of a new state legislature.[17] Among the legislature's first actions was the election of five delegates to the Continental Congress, three of whom were connected with the college at Princeton—Richard Stockton* of the Class of 1748, Francis Hopkinson, an honorary alumnus of the college, and President Witherspoon. Witherspoon was now well-known among the colonials for his patriotic sentiment. Even the British recognized Witherspoon's importance to the revolutionary cause; in July 1776, British troops quartered on Long Island burned Witherspoon in effigy.[18] In the heady days of late June and early July 1776, he took active part in the independence debates in Philadelphia.[19] With other delegates to the Congress, he affixed his signature to the final draft of the Declaration of Independence.

Witherspoon's service to the nation continued throughout the revolutionary period: He served as a member of Congress until December 1779, and again from December 1780 to May 1782; he was deeply involved in the peace negotiations with the British and the French; and he participated actively in the debates that led to the formulation of the Articles of Confederation. Although

Witherspoon was a prominent participant in political questions of the day, his contributions to Presbyterian theology in the revolutionary and early national periods should not be overlooked. Chief among these was his adherence to one variant of Scottish enlightenment thought known as "common sense" philosophy.

One of the most important legacies of the Enlightenment was the work of the Scottish philosopher David Hume. Using the philosophical work of John Locke as a starting point, Hume moved in radical new directions and developed a sharp critique of traditional Christian faith. In his *An Essay Concerning Human Understanding*, published in 1690, Locke denied the notion that the mind was endowed with innate knowledge of any sort. For him, the mind was like "white paper, void of all characters."[20] Knowledge came to the mind in the form of ideas, and ideas were given their shape only by experience. Despite the fact that this scheme found wide acceptance among philosophers, the system was not without its liabilities. The chief difficulty of the Lockean epistemology arose when one searched for bridges between the idea of a thing in the mind and the thing itself as it existed in the real world. And just here, Hume entered the conversation. Hume affirmed Locke's notions of ideas and experience, but gave the system an ironic twist. Because the mind cannot conceive of anything except that which has been experienced, Hume argued, facts cannot be granted credibility a priori. For something to be true, it must have been experienced, otherwise, statements about its truth are mere speculation. The traditional beliefs about cause and effect, under Hume's construction, fell to the ground. For Hume, the relationship between what is called a cause and what is called an effect was a product of the mind; we cannot know whether it has a real existence in the physical world. With one stroke, then, Hume seemed to break the connection between a cause and an effect, and in so doing, attacked the foundations of traditional Christian orthodoxy. Miracles, divine revelation, in short, any proposition that depended on a cause and effect argument, now requires strictly empirical demonstration in order to be verified.[21]

Reactions to Hume's skepticism among Christian theologians came from several quarters, but perhaps the most interesting for Presbyterians was the work of the Scot Thomas Reid. Unlike Hume, Reid insisted that general notions of cause and effect were reliable and that the ideas delivered to the mind by the senses were trustworthy. Under this construction, a person's common sense was a powerful means for discerning the presence of the divine in the world. Witherspoon became familiar with Reid's defense of traditional epistemology during his early years in Scotland, and soon after his arrival in Princeton, began to drive Humean skepticism from the college curriculum. Due in large measure to Witherspoon's influence in the colonies, common sense thought became popular among political philosophers of the revolutionary era, and exerted a powerful influence among Reformed theologians for over a century.[22]

In sum, the Presbyterian contribution to the shaping of the intellectual culture of the new nation cannot be disputed. Witherspoon, together with a host of prominent Presbyterians—William Livingston of New York, publisher of the *Independent Reflector*; Charles Thomson, an elder who served as secretary to the Continental Congress; Joseph Clark and James Armstrong, future moderators of the General Assembly who served as military officers—all were active participants in the political debates leading up to the political separation from Britain, in the military conflict itself, and in the difficult years of national self-scrutiny that ended with the ratification of the United States Constitution in 1789. As one Anglican loyalist, Dr. Charles Inglis, rector of Trinity Church in New York City, noted during the crucial year of 1776, "I do not know one Presbyterian minister, nor have I been able, after strict inquiry, to hear of any who did not by preaching and every effort in their power promote all the measures of the Continental Congress, however extravagant."[23]

THE FIRST GENERAL ASSEMBLY

The spirit of patriotism and the nascent nationalism that had energized the colonists throughout their struggle to form a new nation did not wane in the years following the successful Revolution. Buoyed by their remarkable victory over the world's most powerful empire, and charged with a growing sense of national destiny, Americans tackled a host of social, political, and cultural problems with remarkable energy. Predictably, as the nation began this process of self-definition, so also did the churches begin to probe the meaning of national sovereignty. To be sure, Presbyterians knew what it meant to be Presbyterian. The history of the presbyterian tradition, its creeds, its ecclesial structure, its educational institutions, its social character—all these things could be drawn upon to define the core of Presbyterian Protestantism. As the nation itself probed the meaning of its existence and began to chart its course into the future, however, Presbyterians were faced with a puzzling new question: What did it mean to be an *American* Presbyterian? The political ethos of the early Republic was partly responsible for the immediacy of this query, but rapid institutional changes— congregational growth, geographic expansion, and the administrative inadequacies of the existing single synod system—also helped to focus the problem.

In 1774 concerned clergy began to forward proposals designed to attend to these difficulties.[24] One such plan, for instance, called for the reorganization of the synod into three smaller synods, each of which would be comprised of presbyteries and congregations drawn from a particular region. Some of the plans for recasting the denomination met with rather tepid responses from the rank-and-file clergy and simply dropped from sight; others were postponed due to the exigencies of the Revolution. By 1785, however, with the war finished, it was evident that the administrative structure of the Synod of New York and Philadelphia simply could not cope with the changing complexion of American Presbyterianism. During several of the annual synod meetings in the two decades preceding 1785, for instance, less than 30 percent of the clergy was able to attend, despite the fact that they were required to do so. Hence, the leaders of the church began to formulate plans for a national, representative body that would serve as an effective capstone of the church's administrative hierarchical structure. Despite the near universal perception of the need to restructure the denomination, the planners immediately were confronted with difficulties. Some ministers were highly suspicious of a national body that, in their view, would amass power and thereby usurp the authority of the presbyteries. Among those who recognized the need for a national structure, debates soon erupted about the formation of such a system of ecclesiastical government. Matthew Wilson designed an entirely new form of government, while Samuel Stanhope Smith,* Witherspoon's colleague and eventual successor at the College of New Jersey, argued for the adoption of the system of government and discipline used by the Presbyterian Church in Scotland. Both plans were rejected, and in 1786 the synod selected and empowered a special committee to draft a plan of government.

In May 1787, the synod heard the report of the committee, and after considerable debate received their newly drafted plan and sent it on the presbyteries for formal ratification. The synod also took up two other matters of import. The first concerned amendments to the Confession of Faith and the Directory of Worship. This task was delegated to a committee charged with reshaping the documents and gathering them into a comprehensive instrument for use in the churches. In the main, the new statement paralleled the original Westminster documents and those used in the Scottish churches. The greatest departure from the older documents, however, was found in the American church's understanding of the power and autonomy of the presbytery. Whereas in the British and Scottish churches the General Assembly was the locus of ecclesial authority, the American church raised the importance of the presbytery; synods and the General Assembly were merely "agencies for unifying the life of the Church, considering appeals, and promoting the general welfare of the Church as a whole."[25] The second important issue treated by the synod concerned the division of the synod into four bodies, all of which would be organized under the authority of the General Assembly. A last minute overture deferred this task for yet another year.

In May 1788, the synod held its final meeting. After lengthy consideration the assembled ministers and elders endorsed the reports of the committees and resolved that "the Form of Government and Discipline and the Confession of Faith, as now ratified, is to continue to be our constitution and the confession of our faith and practice unalterable, unless two thirds of the Presbyteries under the care of the General Assembly shall propose alterations or amendments, and such alterations or amendments shall be agreed to and enacted by the General Assembly."[26] Accordingly, the first General Assembly of the Presbyterian Church in the United States of America was held in May 1789 at the Second Presbyterian Church of Philadelphia. The work of the Assembly was divided among 4 synods (New York and New Jersey, Philadelphia, Virginia, and the Carolinas), which were comprised of 16 presbyteries, 177 ministers, 111 probationers, and 419 congregations.[27]

It is of some interest to note that during the same week that the first General

Assembly was convened in Philadelphia, the first Congress of the United States was at work in New York City. Some historians—and not a few of Presbyterian conviction—have claimed this as evidence that there were intentional parallels between Presbyterian polity and the federal system of government enshrined in the United States Constitution. Under this sort of analysis, the Presbyterian tradition becomes both the archetypal American denomination and is credited with an extraordinary influence in the early national period of American history. Although other bits of circumstantial data may suggest the plausibility of such an interpretation (e.g., the prominence of John Witherspoon in the church and in the Continental Congress) most critical historians reject the thesis as unwarranted. What can be said is that both colonial Presbyterians and the nation's earliest political leaders were familiar with Enlightenment political theories common in Revolutionary America, and that both groups descended—genetically and/or intellectually—from progressive political theorists of Scotland and England.[28]

PRESBYTERIANS AND THE STATE

The Presbyterian Church in the United States of America, like other denominations in the post–Revolutionary era, quickly discovered the need for new ways of thinking about religious liberty and the relationship between religion and the state. During the Revolutionary era, every state had redefined its church–state policies; nonetheless, nine of the thirteen states retained officially established religions. After the adoption of the Bill of Rights in 1791, and despite the fact that the First Amendment declared that "Congress shall make no law respecting an establishment of religion, or prohibiting the free exercise thereof," the question of the formal establishment of religion was far from settled in the states. Several issues contributed to this diversity of opinion. Different theorists attached entirely different meanings to the word "establishment": Some believed it to mean what it had in post–Reformation Europe, while others equated establishment with any governmental financial aid to religion.[29] Moreover, different regions of the nation favored different forms of Protestantism, each of which had distinctive views (based largely on their own historical development) of the merits and liabilities of established religion. Finally, even in regions where one form of Protestantism enjoyed hegemony—in New England, for example, where Congregationalism was firmly entrenched—different states handled the problem of establishment in different ways.[30]

Over the course of the colonial era and well into the early national period, Presbyterian leaders were involved in attempts to develop a political ethic that would suit the changing needs of the church. Their participation in the political struggles surrounding the church–state issue in New England was rather limited, primarily because Presbyterianism had failed to establish a foothold in the region. In Connecticut and Massachusetts, for instance, a long and bitter political struggle pitted Baptists and other "dissenters" against the Congregationalist "Standing Order." In Connecticut, the Congregationalist hegemony was broken in 1818;

in Massachusetts, however, legal vestiges of the old Puritan way remained intact until 1833.

In the mid-Atlantic states, however, an entirely different set of circumstances prevailed. Whereas New England Congregationalists and Virginia Anglicans were eventually forced by law to embrace disestablishment, Protestants in Pennsylvania, New York, and New Jersey were long accustomed to living in a situation of denominational pluralism. Presbyterians, Quakers, Dutch Reformed, Anglicans, and Baptists coexisted more or less peaceably in the region. Several factors contributed to this ecumenical spirit, not least of which was the Revolution itself. Because the region suffered enormous losses of property during the war, denominational groups shared sanctuaries, provided financial resources for destitute congregations, and lent clergy across denominational lines. These ecumenical endeavors paid handsome political benefits; in New York, for instance, the disestablishment of Anglicanism occurred quite peacefully.[31]

Although Presbyterians played relatively small parts in hammering out church–state settlements in New England and the mid-Atlantic region, they played a major role in the church–state drama as it was played out in the American South. As early as 1752, Samuel Davies, who was instrumental in establishing Presbyterianism in the American South, drafted an appeal designed to secure religious liberty for Presbyterians who dissented from Virginia's official establishment of Anglicanism.[32] Appealing to the English Act of Toleration, and seeking the good will of the bishop of London, Davies helped to legitimize religious dissent in Virginia. Indeed, by 1759 Anglican attempts to restrict Presbyterianism were largely abandoned.[33]

Ensuring that dissenters could worship in peace was only a part of the challenge facing American Christians in the eighteenth century. The notion that one religion could be officially recognized by the state, even though dissenters were permitted to worship as they pleased, remained a commonly held opinion throughout most of the century. In Virginia, where this idea had long held sway, several events during the revolutionary period involving Virginia Presbyterians finally forced the collapse of the Anglican establishment. In 1776, as Virginia struggled to form a new state government, the legislature passed a Declaration of Rights. The document equivocated on the church–state matter by allowing the Anglican establishment to remain intact even as it recognized the rights of dissenting religious bodies. Although this may have appeared to have been a device to satisfy Virginia's powerful pro-establishment party, Presbyterian and Baptist dissenters viewed it as the first successful breach in the hitherto impregnable fortress of Anglican legal preferment. Indeed, the dissenters' sanguine interpretation of the Declaration was quickly borne out; later that same year the Virginia House of Delegates enacted legislation "that exempted dissenters from being taxed to support the Established Church and suspended the payment of statutory salaries of the clergy."[34] Virginia maintained this difficult middle position between establishment and disestablishment until 1779, when Thomas Jefferson introduced his famous "Bill for Establishing Religious Freedom." The controversy surrounding his proposal led to further delays about the place of religion in the state, which, in the view of many clergy—both established and dissenting—led to a perceptible lapse in public morality. Indeed, Presbyterian leaders in the Hanover Presbytery became so worried about the waning influence of religion that they supported a bill calling for a new version of established religion on a multi-denominational basis.[35] That bill met with defeat after a public outcry, part of which included James Madison's classic "Memorial and Remonstrance." Finally, in 1786 the House enacted Jefferson's bill, which permanently settled the church–state question in Virginia.

In 1781 the Synod of Philadelphia and New York had "solemnly and publicly" declared that the church renounced "the principles of intolerance" and expressed its belief "that every peaceable member of civil society ought to be protected in the full and free exercise of their religion."[36] Although Presbyterians had briefly toyed with the idea of participating in an inclusive Virginia settlement, in every region of the nation they had remained faithful to their self-confessed ideals of religious toleration and had been the friends of disestablishment. The close of the eighteenth century found American Presbyterianism prosperous indeed; the church had successfully weathered the storms of immigration, institutional organization, the American Revolution, and the establishment of religious freedom.

This institutional well-being would be tested in the decades to come, however. Just over the horizon stood a series of intractable problems—union with the Congregationalists, another "great awakening," the need for social reform, the problem of slavery, the Civil War, and Charles Darwin—that would change the course of Presbyterianism in America.

NOTES

1. Quoted in William Warren Sweet, *Makers of Christianity from John Cotton to Lyman Abbott* (New York: Henry Holt & Co., 1937), p. 25.

2. Leonard J. Trinterud, *The Forming of an American Tradition: A Re-examination of Colonial Presbyterianism* (Philadelphia: Westminster Press, 1949), pp. 34–35.

3. Quoted in Trinterud, *American Tradition*, p. 46.

4. For more extensive treatments of the subscription controversy and the settlement in 1729, see Bryan F. LeBeau, "The Subscription Controversy and Jonathan Dickinson," *Journal of Presbyterian History* 54 (Fall 1976), 317–335, and Milton J. Coalter, Jr., *Gilbert Tennent, Son of Thunder: A Case Study of Continental Pietism's Impact on the First Great Awakening in the Middle Colonies* (Westport, Conn.: Greenwood Press, 1986), pp. 29–36.

5. Quoted in Trinterud, *American Tradition*, p. 57. For a substantive analysis of Gilbert Tennent's relationships with Dutch Pietism, see Coalter, *Gilbert Tennent, Son of Thunder*.

6. Quoted in Trinterud, *American Tradition*, p. 91.

7. Ibid., p. 107.

8. Ibid., p. 121.

9. For statistical data on the growth of Presbyterianism in America, see Edwin S. Gaustad, *Historical Atlas of Religion in America*, rev. ed. (New York: Harper and Row, 1976).

10. See Alison B. Olson, "The Founding of Princeton University: Religion and Politics in Eighteenth-Century New Jersey," *New Jersey History* 87 (1969), 133–150.

11. On the early history of this Old Side Presbyterian institution, see George Morgan, "The Colonial Origin of Newark Academy," *Delaware Notes* 8 (1934), 7–30; George H. Ryden, "The Newark Academy of Delaware in Colonial Days," *Pennsylvania History* 2 (October 1935), 205–224.

12. For details of the Old Side intrigue, see Trinterud, *American Tradition*, pp. 218–219.

13. The loyalist, conservative, radical typology is developed in ibid., pp. 242ff.

14. These examples of student revolutionary activity are cited in Thomas Jefferson Wertenbaker, *Princeton: 1746–1896* (Princeton, N.J.: Princeton University Press, 1946), pp. 56ff.

15. Trinterud, *American Tradition*, p. 243.

16. John Witherspoon, "The Dominion of Providence" (Philadelphia, 1776). The sermon is quoted in Nathan O. Hatch, *The Sacred Cause of Liberty: Republican Thought and the Millennium in Revolutionary New England* (New Haven, Conn.: Yale University Press, 1977), p. 63, n. 20.

17. For further details of Witherspoon's role in the ouster of Governor Franklin, see Wertenbaker, *Princeton*, pp. 87ff., and Varnum Lansing Collins, *President Witherspoon: A Biography*, 2 vols. (Princeton, N.J.: Princeton University Press, 1925), 1:204ff.

18. Trinterud, *American Tradition*, p. 243.

19. For further details on Witherspoon's participation in the drafting of the Declaration, see Collins, *President Witherspoon*, 1:219–221, n. 17.

20. John Locke, "An Essay Concerning Human Understanding" in *Locke's Essays: An Essay Concerning Human Understanding and A Treatise on the Conduct of the Understanding* (Philadelphia: Kay & Troutman, 1847), p. 75.

21. For a full discussion of Hume's thought, see V. C. Chappell, *The Philosophy of David Hume*, The Modern Library of the World's Best Books (New York: Random House, 1963), pp. vii–lxvii, and Angus J. Mackay, "David Hume," in *Philosophers of the Enlightenment*, ed. Peter Gilmour (Totowa, N.J.: Barnes & Noble Books, 1990), pp. 63–73.

22. For more detailed accounts of Common Sense Philosophy see Sydney E. Ahlstrom, "The Scottish Philosophy and American Theology," *Church History* 24 (1955), 257–272; Mark A. Noll, "Common Sense Traditions and American Evangelical Thought," *American Quarterly* 37 (1985), 216–238; and Henry F. May, *The Enlightenment in America* (New York: Oxford University Press, 1976).

23. Lefferts A. Loetscher, *A Brief History of the Presbyterians*, 3d ed. (Philadelphia: Westminster Press, 1978), p. 75.

24. For an extended treatment of the negotiations leading up to the first General Assembly, see Trinterud, *American Tradition*, pp. 279ff.

25. Ibid., p. 299. Ibid., pp. 296ff., treats the differences between the American and Scottish creedal documents at some length.

26. Quoted in Trinterud, *American Tradition*, p. 295.

27. The statistical data are found in Loetscher, *Brief History*, p. 77.

28. Loetscher, *Brief History*, pp. 77–78, offers a judicious caution against making unwarranted claims about these similarities.

29. For an extended treatment of the various understandings of the term "establishment," see Leonard W. Levy, *The Establishment Clause: Religion and the First Amendment* (New York: Macmillan, 1986).

30. Thomas J. Curry, *The First Freedoms: Church and State in America to the Passage of the First Amendment* (New York: Oxford University Press, 1986) is a useful general treatment of the church–state issue in early America.

31. For an extended treatment of the situation in revolutionary New York, see Richard W. Pointer, *Protestant Pluralism and the New York Experience: A Study of Eighteenth-Century Religious Diversity* (Bloomington and Indianapolis: Indiana University Press, 1988).

32. Excerpts from Davies's epistle may be consulted in John F. Wilson and Donald L. Drakeman, eds., *Church and State in American History*, 2d ed. (Boston: Beacon Press, 1987), pp. 38–42.

33. Rhys Isaac, *The Transformation of Virginia, 1740–1790* (Chapel Hill: University of North Carolina Press, 1982), p. 153.

34. Ibid., p. 281.

35. See ibid., pp. 283–284. Loetscher, *Brief History*, pp. 75–76, denies that Virginia Presbyterians leaned toward such a multi-denominational establishment.

36. Quoted in Loetscher, *Brief History*, p. 76.

3
NORTHERN PRESBYTERIANISM IN THE NINETEENTH CENTURY

Having settled, finally, on an organizational structure that would sustain a growing and diversifying denomination, American Presbyterians, like others in the new nation, turned to the building of institutions early in the nineteenth century. Those institutions would serve both to define and to sustain American Presbyterianism, still very much in its formative period. When the German-born historian Philip Schaff made his mid-century assessment of religion in America, he observed that Presbyterianism "is without question one of the most numerous, respectable, worthy, intelligent, and influential denominations, and has a particularly strong hold on the solid middle class."[1]

Whatever the number and intelligence of its adherents, much of the strength and prominence Presbyterianism enjoyed derived from the resilience of its institutions. At the same time, however, Presbyterian institutions—like those in every other American denomination—were buffeted by the winds of theological and sectional controversy during what was to be a very turbulent century. A single denomination in 1800 divided into at least half a dozen different, often contentious, strands by century's end.

PRESBYTERIANS AND REVIVAL

For Presbyterians, as for other American Protestants, the nineteenth century got off to a rousing start with a series of revivals that, taken together, comprised what has been called the "Second Great Awakening." These revivals eventually encompassed three geographical theaters of the new nation—New England, the Cumberland Valley, and western New York—and they had an enormous effect on both the religious and social life in the frontier areas, especially in the South. Missionaries distributed Bibles and religious tracts, evangelists proclaimed the salvific merits of faith in Christ, and new congregations were founded. Benevolent societies formed rapidly within religious communities, and a host of social ills were targeted for reform. Alcohol consumption, utterly prodigious by today's standards, abated in the wake of revival as preachers emphasized the importance of personal holiness. Religious reformers also attacked dueling, prostitution, and chattel slavery.

A Presbyterian preacher from North Carolina, James McGready,* was an important figure in the Cumberland revival. In 1796, facing opposition at home for his virulent revival preaching, McGready headed west and began preaching at various gatherings on the frontier. Under the influence of McGready and other preachers, the revival fires soon spread. The Gaspar River and Cane Ridge camp meetings attracted many thousands of seekers, and hundreds returned home converted. Many Presbyterians, however, took a dim view of some of the infamous revival excesses of the Kentucky awakening and looked askance at the theology that undergirded revival preaching, a theology that emphasized human initiative in the salvation process rather than an abject reliance on the unmerited grace of God. David Rice, a Presbyterian minister in Kentucky, even opined that the religious anarchy at Cane Ridge had some connection with the French Revolution. Under increasing pressure to bring their preaching into line with strict Reformed doctrines, disgruntled members of the Cumberland Presbytery withdrew from the Synod of Kentucky in 1810 and formed what became the Cumberland Presbyterian Church.[2]

Those who insisted on a rigid adherence to Reformed theology, however, faced an even stiffer challenge in the North. The opening of the Erie Canal in 1825 provided farmers in western New York access to eastern markets and set off an economic boom along the western reaches of the 341-mile waterway. Soon religion began to boom as well; revival fires erupted with such fervor and frequency in places like Auburn, Rome, and Utica that the region earned the sobriquet "the burned-over district." No one stoked those fires more insistently and systematically than Charles Grandison Finney,* who was ordained to the ministry by the St. Lawrence Presbytery on 1 July 1824, at which time he conceded that he had never even read the Westminster Confession of Faith. Finney, trained as an attorney, had little patience for the theological niceties of orthodox Calvinism. In contrast to Jonathan Edwards, whose account of the Northampton revival during the First Great Awakening was titled *A Faithful Narrative of a Surprising Work of God*, Finney believed that revivals were the work of people and that if an evangelist followed the proper procedures, which Finney outlined in *Lectures on Revivals of Religion* in 1835, he could expect a revival. Suppose, said Finney, that a minister was to preach the Calvinist version of divine sovereignty among farmers busy about the task of sowing their grain. "Let him tell them that God is a sovereign, and will give them a crop only when it pleases him, and that for them to plow and plant and labor as if they expected to raise a crop is very wrong, and taking the work out of the hands of God, that it interferes with his sovereignty, and is going on in their own strength; and that there is no connection between the means and the result on which they can depend. And now, suppose the farmers should believe such doctrine. Why, they would starve the world to death." Harvesting souls, Finney insisted, was like harvesting grain. A spiritual awakening, he declared, "is not a miracle, or dependent on a miracle, in any sense. It is a purely philosophical result of the right use of the constituted means—as much so as any other effect produced by the application of means."[3] Finney's techniques, which he called "new measures," included the use of media to publicize meetings, exhortations by women assistants, protracted nightly services, and the anxious bench, where auditors troubled about the state of their souls could seek counsel and wrestle with their eternal destinies.

Finney was also an accomplished and persuasive orator, arguing his case for conversion with a lawyerly precision that frequently elicited anguished cries for salvation. The revival in Rochester in 1831 marked the zenith of his revival career and his influence as an evangelist. Some 350 new church members were added to the rolls of Rochester's three Presbyterian churches.[4] Because of his adroit use of newspapers, moreover, Finney's renown and influence spread far beyond western New York, and during his later years at Oberlin College he estimated that 100,000 people became church members nationwide as a consequence of the Rochester revival.

NEW SCHOOL AND OLD SCHOOL

The activities of Finney and likeminded evangelists, however, soon precipitated a schism among American Presbyterians. The exaltation of free will and self-determinism that marked Finney's theology had an unmistakable appeal to a people that had just taken their political destiny into their own hands and who were now inebriated with Jacksonian democracy and the frontier spirit of rugged individualism. Traditional, old line Calvinistic notions about innate depravity and divine election were no longer popular, nor did they lend themselves easily to revivals. Those within the Presbyterian church who wished to brook no compromise on Calvinistic doctrines came to be known as Old School Presbyterians, and in the 1830s they plotted to take action against what became known as the New School faction. Finney himself chose to leave Presbyterianism altogether in 1835, but not before firing a parting shot. "No doubt there is a jubilee in hell every year," he wrote in *Lectures on Revivals of Religion*, "about the time of the meeting of the General Assembly."[5]

Ever since the General Assembly of 1831 the Old School had sought to enforce doctrinal conformity, but found itself outnumbered by New School forces.[6] In 1835, for instance, they circulated an "Act and Testimony" over the signatures of Old Schoolers that warned of "the prevalence of unsound doctrine and laxity in discipline."[7] Indeed, a large array of issues were involved in the Old School–New School controversies. In 1801 Presbyterians had joined with Congregationalists in an extraordinary act of cooperation known as the Plan of Union. Faced with the rapid growth of population in frontier areas to the West, Presbyterians and Congregationalists decided to pool their mission efforts in order to avoid unnecessary duplication. Such a plan seemed eminently sensible, but for the conservatives of the Old School it opened the door to theological laxity because the Congregationalists did not require formal subscription to the Westminster standards, and the Plan of Union therefore admitted Congregationalist ministers who had never affirmed Westminster through the back door of "Union" pulpits. The Old School, moreover, became jealous of denominational prerogatives and grew suspicious of the Plan of Union because it compromised the distinctives of Presbyterian doctrine and polity. The most important factor in the growing tensions, however, was that the Old School looked askance at the revivals in general and especially at the underlying doctrinal innovations of Finney and Nathaniel William Taylor, a Congregationalist minister, both of whom had moderated Calvinist views of utter depravity and inability to accommodate human volition in the salvation process.

In 1835 Albert Barnes,* a minister at First Presbyterian Church in Philadelphia and a graduate of Princeton Seminary, published a commentary on the book of Romans that the Old School Synod of Philadelphia charged, denied the doctrine of original sin and taught that the unregenerate could keep the commandments and initiate their own conversions. Suspended from the ministry for a year by the synod, Barnes appealed to the General Assembly in 1836. After a two-week trial the Assembly, with a majority New School representation, acquitted Barnes. Incensed at this affront to orthodox Calvinism, Old School activists organized a "Committee of Correspondence" and insisted upon separation. At the General Assembly of 1837 the Old School finally mustered a majority and formally abrogated the 1801 Plan of Union with the Congregationalists, the putative source of these doctrinal innovations. The Old Schoolers declared, moreover, that those synods organized under the Plan of Union were illegal, and they thereby exscinded the Synods of Western Reserve, Utica, Genessee, and Geneva because of their "Congregational" origins and New School sympathies.

The New School, stunned by this development, regrouped in Auburn, New York, at what became known as the Auburn Convention. They refused to accept the excisions, resolved to remain Presbyterian, and insisted that the disowning acts of the 1837 Assembly were null and void. During the meeting of the 1838 General Assembly at the Seventh Presbyterian Church in Philadelphia, New School representatives sought recognition by the Old School moderator, who promptly denied it. Chaos ensued, and, amid the shouts and the tumult, the New School declared itself a "Constitutional Assembly" and voted to adjourn to a more hospitable location. Both groups held their meetings in Philadelphia, albeit at different venues, and both bodies claimed the name "The Presbyterian Church in the United States of America."

The New School–Old School schism rent the fabric of American Presbyterianism. While the majority of the New School group came from upstate New York and the Western Reserve, it also claimed the allegiance of the Synods of Michigan and Eastern Tennessee. In addition, the New School attracted substantial numbers in New Jersey, Indiana, Illinois, and Ohio. Many presbyteries and many congregations were bitterly divided by the New School–Old School acrimony; in at least one case rival factions of a congregation physically divided their meetinghouse and hauled one half to a new location.[8] The New School, on the whole, lamented the schism. The Old School, however, insisted that such a purge was necessary in order to safeguard both denominational prerogatives and what they viewed as the essentials of Reformed doctrine, even though they lost about four-ninths of their membership.

THEOLOGICAL EDUCATION

For some time a number of Presbyterians had recognized the importance of theological education as a means of both preserving and propagating Reformed doctrine. At the May 1808 meeting of the Presbyterian General Assembly, Archibald Alexander,* the young pastor of Philadelphia's Pine Street Church and the Assembly's retiring moderator, delivered a stirring sermon calling for the establishment of theological seminaries "in every presbytery, or at least every synod." "If you would have a well-disciplined army," Alexander told the Assembly, "you must begin by appointing good officers." The system of education in existing colleges and universities, he thought, was not up to the task of preparing ministers: "The great extension of the physical sciences, and the taste and fashion of the age, have given such a shape and direction to the academical discourse, that, I confess, it appears to me to be little adapted to introduce a youth to the study of sacred scriptures." Alexander identified what he considered the twin threats to evangelical truth: "rational Christianity" on the one hand, and "enthusiasm" on the other. Any proposed seminary would have to avoid those two extremes. "The end of all our labours . . . should be to promote holiness in the great body of the church," he concluded. "The necessity of purity of heart and life, in order to salvation, is indispensable."[9]

Such concerns were not new among Presbyterians. The College of New Jersey had been established by New Side Presbyterians in 1746 largely in order to educate clergy sympathetic to the revival. As early as 1775 Jacob Green of New Jersey had advocated special schools for aspiring ministers. In 1801 Alexander had resigned the presidency of Hampden–Sydney College in Virginia to undertake an extended tour of New England. In the course of his travels Alexander became concerned about the state of theological education in America, especially among Presbyterians. Ministerial training in the colonies had been, by and large, rather haphazard. Typically, an aspiring cleric would study privately with an ordained minister, a kind of apprentice system that gave rise to a great deal of theological diversity and even confusion. After he resumed the presidency at Hampden–Sydney the following year, Alexander continued to ponder the problem of theological education, and those ruminations soon evolved into agitations for a Presbyterian seminary.

Ashbel Green* of Philadelphia's Second Presbyterian Church and Samuel Miller,* a Presbyterian minister in New York City, shared Alexander's concerns.

As early as March 1805 Green and Miller had corresponded about the dire shortage of qualified clergy. Perhaps just as important to the designs of a Presbyterian seminary was the example of Andover Theological Seminary. Stung by the appointment of Henry Ware, a Unitarian, to the Hollis Chair of Divinity at Harvard, Trinitarian Congregationalists in New England organized Andover in 1808 as a counter to Harvard's "apostasy" and as the first institution in America devoted entirely to the training of clergy.

The final motivation behind the establishment of a Presbyterian seminary lay in a growing disaffection with the College of New Jersey, known today as Princeton University. Although the college had ably served the educational needs of the Presbyterian ministry in its early years, its production of ministers had fallen off dramatically by the opening of the nineteenth century. John Witherspoon* had brought an uncommon energy to his tenure as the college's president. His efforts secured for Princeton both a financial stability and a prominence that set the college on a par with the older New England institutions of Harvard and Yale. But Witherspoon's rejection of philosophical idealism and his dogmatic attachment to the tenets of Scottish common sense realism left a lasting mark on the college and on American Presbyterian theology. While ostensibly maintaining Presbyterianism's commitment to the theological tradition that reached back to Augustine, Calvin, and the Puritan William Ames, Witherspoon's modifications to the college curriculum and to the composition of its faculty moved the college in new directions. The hallmarks of the older tradition, a stress on innate depravity and the need for supernatural revelation, gave way to the more progressive notions; human agency was elevated and given new credibility, and the science of moral philosophy took center stage in the curriculum.

Witherspoon's presence and power was so great, however, that the adjustments he made became apparent only after his death in 1794, when his hapless successor, Samuel Stanhope Smith,* was forced to wrestle with the theological, intellectual, and ecclesiastical tensions bequeathed by his own mentor. Smith faced a number of vexing questions. Could Princeton simultaneously accommodate rigorous scientific and traditional Christian piety? Or did new canons of critical inquiry work against a distinctly Christian world view? Could the college train both statesmen and ministers? Or would the college become increasingly involved in politics and the larger cultural issues at the expense of the distinctly Christian education? By the turn of the century it appeared as if the college had turned from the needs of the faithful to the problems of the nation at large. The example of Witherspoon's tireless engagement with the Revolution, together with his distinguished service in the Continental Congress, the New Jersey legislature, and with various related civic causes, had inspired many a college graduate to choose service to the nation over service to the Lord. From 1776 to 1783 only seventeen Princeton students became ministers, 21 percent of the graduates; from 1784 to 1794, Witherspoon's final ten years, the percentage dropped to 13.[10]

This did not sit well with some Presbyterian clergy. When Smith caught wind of efforts to organize a seminary in 1806, he sought to stop the movement toward the formation of an independent seminary by outlining the advantages of the college for the preparation of ministers. Alexander, Green, and Miller were not persuaded, and in 1809 the Presbytery of Philadelphia, at Green's behest, asked the General Assembly to form a theological school. The following year the Assembly chose Miller to head an exploratory committee, which, after canvassing the presbyteries, proposed a central seminary under the control of the General Assembly. The committee selected Green to draft a constitution for the seminary, which was approved by the 1811 Assembly with minor revisions.

The "Plan of the Theological Seminary" stipulated that graduates of the proposed seminary would have studied the original languages of the Bible, would be conversant with church history and "the principal arguments and writings relative to what has been called the deistical controversy," and would be able to support the Westminster Standards "by a ready, pertinent, and abundant quotation of Scripture texts for that purpose." The purpose of the seminary was "to form men for the Gospel ministry, who shall truly believe, and cordially love, and therefore endeavour to propagate and defend, in all its genuineness, simplicity, and fullness, that system of religious belief and practice which is set forth in the Confession of Faith, Catechisms, and Plan of Government and Discipline of the Presbyterian Church."[11]

The trustees of Princeton College still opposed the plan for a separate seminary and offered, in effect, to revamp the curriculum so "that the principal direction of the college in its instruction, government, and discipline, be gradually turned to promote the objects of the theological institution."[12] President Smith reviewed the advantages to prospective ministers of specialized theological training in the context of undergraduate life, including "the emulation and encouragement communicated by a variety of fellow students, the opportunity of cultivating any branch of science, and an access at all times to a large and well selected theological library."[13]

By then, however, the call for a separate institution had gained a momentum of its own. Presbyterian officials, moreover, were not moved by Smith's arguments because the college refused to surrender its autonomy to the General Assembly; it would still be governed by a self-perpetuating board. Furthermore, they imbibed serious suspicions about the college as a hotbed of student disorder, especially after student riots over living conditions and harsh discipline led to the temporary suspension of 125 out of the college's 200 students in 1807. After negotiations with the college trustees, however, Alexander and his colleagues decided to locate the seminary in Princeton. The college granted the seminary the use of college facilities and agreed not to hire a professor of theology as long as the seminary remained in Princeton. (The college's theology professor, Henry Kollock, had resigned in 1806 because the number of undergraduates interested in theology was "so small as to render by labours of little consequences.")[14]

The General Assembly, which retained control over the seminary, elected

Alexander as professor of ''Didactic and Polemic Theology.'' Alexander's inauguration and the official opening of ''The Theological Seminary of the Presbyterian Church in the United States of America at Princeton, New Jersey'' took place on 12 August 1812 in Princeton's First Presbyterian Church. Three students studied under Alexander, the school's sole professor, that first year. In 1813 the General Assembly voted to keep the seminary in Princeton and to accept an offer of land from Richard Stockton,* Presbyterian layman and one of the signers of the Declaration of Independence. Five additional students came the second year, and Miller joined Alexander on the faculty as Professor of Ecclesiastical History and Church Government.

Under the influence Alexander, Miller, and especially Charles Hodge,* one of the school's early graduates who was appointed professor of Oriental and biblical literature in 1822, Princeton Theological Seminary became the leading defender of orthodox Calvinism and Old School Presbyterianism in the nineteenth century. In an oft-quoted phrase delivered at the semicentennial celebration of his professorate, Hodge noted, ''I am not afraid to say that a new idea never originated in this Seminary,'' an indication of his conviction that the Princetonians stood firmly within the ambit of their Protestant forebears.[15] Echoing a similar sentiment at the seminary's centennial in 1912, President Francis Landey Patton* declared that the ''theological position of Princeton Seminary is exactly the same today that it was a hundred years ago'' in its fidelity to the ''distinctive content of the Reformed Theology.''[16] Although these claims have often been cited as evidence of the seminary's attachment to a conservative, even antiquated, theology, this sort of critique is an oversimplification. During the course of the nineteenth century the seminary emerged as the most prominent Presbyterian institution in the nation. Given its prominent role, even after the New School–Old School schism and the subsequent North–South bifurcation of the church during the sectional crisis, the Princetonians keenly felt the need to maintain vital connections with the best of the past. The purveyors of what became known as the ''Princeton theology'' doubtless underestimated the degree to which they served as innovators, and they surely steered toward the rationalistic side of what Alexander had identified as the twin perils of ''enthusiasm'' on the one hand and ''rational Christianity'' on the other. Generations of Princeton theologians (Alexander, Hodge, his son Archibald Alexander Hodge,* and perhaps the greatest intellect of them all, Benjamin Breckinridge Warfield*) tenaciously, and at times eloquently, defended what they regarded as the essentials of Reformed theology amidst a Protestant culture enamored of the Enlightenment, inebriated with self-determinism, and intrigued by the possibilities of Finney's ''new measures.'' The Princeton theologians unequivocally rejected all three, relying heavily on Scottish ''common sense'' realism in the process. The significance of their stand in the theological maelstrom of nineteenth-century America should not be overlooked.

In addition to his three-volume *Systematic Theology* (which, at least until very recently, was still used in conservative seminaries), Charles Hodge edited the

Biblical Repertory and Princeton Review, which became enormously influential as the mouthpiece of Princeton orthodoxy to American Protestantism. The *Princeton Review* (it was known by various names throughout its history) offered lengthy, critical review essays that attacked nineteenth-century theological "innovation" in its various guises, from the New Divinity to Oberlin perfectionism, from Transcendentalism to Arminianism, from the Mercersburg theology to Horace Bushnell. It also offered comment on internal Presbyterian matters as well as on larger national issues, such as slavery and temperance, both of which Hodge opposed.[17]

When the Old School–New School schism ruptured Presbyterian unity in 1837, the *Princeton Review* and Princeton Seminary took up the cudgels of polemicism and emerged as the major apologists for the Old School. By then, however, Princeton's was by no means the only voice of American Presbyterianism. In 1818 Auburn Theological Seminary was founded in Auburn, New York, followed in 1823 by Union Theological Seminary in Virginia, Pennsylvania's Western Seminary in 1827 (whose antecedents lay in the 1780s), and Columbia Seminary in Columbia, South Carolina, in 1828. In the fall of 1832 Lane Theological Seminary began its classes in Walnut Hills, Ohio, a suburb of Cincinnati. Lane had been founded by Old School Presbyterians, but under the direction of its president, the redoubtable Lyman Beecher,* the school began to lean in the direction of activist revivalism. A dispute in 1834 prompted Theodore Dwight Weld and a majority of his fellow students to withdraw from the school, complaining that the institution sought to thwart their abolitionist zeal. After several months on their own, the Lane rebels, as they became known, effectively took over Oberlin College. Asa Mahan, erstwhile trustee at Lane, was designated president, and Finney was elected professor of theology and became the dominant figure there for over forty years. Oberlin remained at least vaguely Presbyterian for most of the nineteenth century, but it was better known for its antislavery efforts, for its emphasis on manual labor as part of the curriculum, and for being the first college in the country to admit women and African-Americans.

During the winter of 1835–36 a group of Presbyterians gathered in New York City to discuss the formation of still another Presbyterian seminary.[18] While some members of the group were sympathetic to what was then emerging as the Old School of Presbyterianism, most organizers of the seminary supported the New School—that is, they shied away from strict subscription to confessional standards, embraced revivalism, and generally emphasized the more experiential, affective dimension of the Reformed tradition. Despite their New School suspicions about the utility of creedal affirmations, the founders of the new seminary required that all professors affirm the following:

I believe the Scriptures of the Old and New Testament to be the word of God, the only infallible rule of faith and practice; and I do now, in the presence of God and the Directors of this Seminary, solemnly and sincerely receive the Westminster Confession of Faith as containing the system of doctrine taught in the Holy Scriptures. I do also, in like manner, approve of the Presbyterian Form of Government; and I do solemnly promise that I will not teach or inculcate anything which shall appear to me to be subversive of said system of doctrines, or of the principles of said Form of Government, so long as I shall continue to be a Professor in the Seminary.[19]

Although the new institution would come to repudiate all of those views before the end of the century, Union Theological Seminary (originally named ''The New York Theological Seminary'') opened its doors in 1836 as a decidedly Presbyterian institution. From the beginning, however, Union retained an independent spirit, and its New School proclivities, which became even more pronounced with the arrival of Henry Boynton Smith* in 1850, soon clashed with the Old School sentiments of the Princeton theologians, fifty-five miles to the southwest.

MISSIONS

The rapid westward expansion of the new nation after 1800 offered American Presbyterians both opportunities and challenges. Presbyterians and New England Congregationalists, whose theology and style of worship were quite similar, both sent missionaries to the frontier of central and western New York. Rather than duplicating organizational structures, they had agreed in 1801 to a proposal by Jonathan Edwards, Jr., to coordinate their mission efforts. These practical considerations were the major force behind the Plan of Union; although the Plan eventually became one of the sources of division in the Old School–New School controversy, it allowed individual congregations early in the nineteenth century to be simultaneously affiliated with both the Congregationalist and the Presbyterian denominations. It also alleviated somewhat the desperate shortage of clergy because any such congregation could be served by a minister of either denomination.

Home missions received considerable attention in the antebellum period. The General Assembly established a Standing Committee of Missions in 1802, which was quickly deluged with appeals for help from central and western New York and from the Ohio and Cumberland valleys, precisely the regions in the throes of revival. The supply of educated clergy could not keep up with the demand, especially in frontier areas. Unlike Baptists and Methodists, who exacted no such requirements, Presbyterians steadfastly insisted on an educated clergy, a stipulation that, in time, would limit their growth on the frontier simply because Presbyterians could not meet the demand for clergy. The Second Great Awakening itself proved divisive, especially in the South where Presbyterian revivalists, impatient with the Calvinistic scruples of Presbyterians in the East, eventually seceded to form the Cumberland Presbyterian Church. American Presbyterians in the North, meanwhile, united with other Protestants in the various reform and benevolent societies emanating from the Second Great Awakening.

Nineteenth-century Presbyterian missions at home received perhaps their greatest impetus from a diminutive man who, upon his graduation from Princeton Seminary in 1858, was rejected as a candidate for foreign missionary service because of his fragile constitution. Sheldon Jackson,* who became known as "The Bishop of All Beyond," turned his attentions instead to the American West, and in the course of a heroic career as a home missionary traveled throughout the West and into Alaska founding churches, organizing Presbyterian missions, and even serving as Alaska's first superintendent of public instruction. Among Eskimos, Jackson is still remembered and appreciated for his daring plan to import reindeer from Lapland and Siberia to provide a stable food supply for native Alaskans.

Presbyterians, following the lead of the Congregationalists, also began to look beyond American horizons. Samuel J. Mills and a number of fellow students at Williams College met near a haystack in 1806 and pledged themselves to missionary service. Several years later many of these students, some of whom had gone to Andover Seminary for further education, offered themselves to the Congregational General Association of Massachusetts as missionaries to foreign lands. The General Association responded in 1810 by forming the American Board of Commissioners for Foreign Service, popularly known as the American Board. In 1811 the Board asked the Presbyterian General Assembly to set up a parallel organization of their own; the Assembly declined, however, preferring, in the spirit of the Plan of Union, simply to cooperate with the American Board. The Congregationalists responded by adding a number of Presbyterians to the Board, thereby cementing an alliance that lasted until 1838, when Presbyterians formed their own Board of Foreign Missions.

THE ERODING CONSENSUS

As noted above, American Presbyterians found themselves divided over several issues during the early decades of the nineteenth century, chief among them the New School–Old School split of 1837. But the issue of slavery provided the occasion for even larger and more profound divisions.[20] Since 1787 Presbyterians had taken notice of the perils of slavery, but they generally advocated a cautious, moderate approach to abolition. The New School was inclined to press the case for abolitionism more forcefully, prompting the succession of its southern constituency in 1857 to form "The United Synod of the Presbyterian Church in the United States of America." The final division occurred during the meeting of the Old School General Assembly in Philadelphia just a few weeks after the attack on Fort Sumter in 1861. Northerners pressed for and finally adopted resolutions upholding the Union, whereupon the southern delegates withdrew. Later that same year, on 4 December, delegates from forty-seven presbyteries in the South organized "The Presbyterian Church in the Confederate States of America," thereby institutionalizing a breach that would not be healed for more than a century.

Theological divisions, though perhaps less apparent, raged as well. The Princeton theologians, led by Charles Hodge, tried valiantly to defend Reformed orthodoxy from the onslaught of Arminian self-determinism, Enlightenment rationalism, Darwinism, and higher criticism. Against evolution, for instance, Hodge argued in *What Is Darwinism?* (1874) that Darwin's theory was merely an unproved hypothesis that could not be reconciled with the "facts" contained in the early chapters of Genesis. It was a pernicious theory, he said, because it sought to account for the development of all organisms through natural causes absent the agency of God. In Hodge's view, Darwin's profession of belief in a creator rang hollow, and Hodge was not at all surprised that the opponents of Christianity had so eagerly embraced Darwin's theory of organic evolution.[21]

Indeed, the theologians at Princeton Seminary frequently regarded themselves as the last line of defense in the battles against unbelief and heresy. "I sincerely join you in praying that this fountain of divine truth may never be poisoned or adulterated with error," Archibald Alexander wrote in a private letter in 1846; "I entertain a strong confidence that this Seminary will continue to teach the pure doctrine of the grace of God to the end of the world."[22] Princeton's weapons in this apocalyptic struggle were a literalistic biblical hermeneutic, Calvinistic theology as filtered through Francis Turretin, a seventeenth-century Protestant scholastic theologian, and hefty doses of Baconianism, with its emphasis on inductive reasoning, and Scottish common sense philosophy.

Much of the Princeton theologians' energies centered around a defense of the Bible, which they believed was under siege by various forces, including Darwin's theories, but especially by the discipline of higher criticism emanating from Germany. The work of the higher critics pointed out internal inconsistencies and contradictions in the Scriptures, called into question the scientific and factual data in the Bible, challenged the traditional authorship of various books, and, in general, cast doubts on the veracity of the Bible. Hodge and other Protestant theologians of the nineteenth century quickly recognized what was at stake in these discussions. For them, the Scriptures contained both the way of salvation and a great deal of accurate information about the created order and humanity's place therein. These theologians were hardly obscurantist in outlook; they had received the finest scholarly training available and had spent their careers seeking to articulate the meaning of biblical faith for their contemporary culture. For them, the Scriptures were the key source in this enterprise. Hence, if the Bible was discredited, they believed, the foundations of Protestant theology would crumble, and the Church's guide to knowledge and truth about life itself would soon come to be ignored.

The Princeton theologians—especially A. A. Hodge and Warfield in an 1881 article titled "Inspiration," published in the *Presbyterian Review*—rushed to the rescue. They insisted that the Bible was inspired and utterly without error in the *original autographs*. It was true, they acknowledged, that errors had crept into the present texts of Scripture, but those were errors of transmission on the part of copyists; they in no way impugned the integrity of the inspired—and flawless—

originals, nor were any of the apparent contradictions of sufficient consequence to lead the present-day believer astray.

The Princeton theologians have been accused of theological innovation in their appeal to the purity of the original autographs in order to deflect the arguments of the higher critics, but that is certainly not the case; contemporaries offered similar arguments, and the doctrine of flawless original autographs dates back to St. Augustine.[23] The Princetonians, however, directed considerable, renewed attention to the argument, and the 1881 article was the first time they put forward such a comprehensive statement devoted solely to the matter of biblical inspiration. In the face of new and decidedly modern attacks on the Bible, moreover, the notion of ''inerrancy'' as propagated by the Princetonians became a defensive position.

Not all Presbyterians agreed with A. A. Hodge and Warfield. The most prominent dissenter was Charles A. Briggs* of Union Theological Seminary in New York. Briggs and Hodge were co-editors of the *Presbyterian Review* when the Hodge-Warfield article was published, but their correspondence at the time indicates a growing strain in their relations and, by extension, between Princeton and Union seminaries. Briggs, a prolific scholar, was appointed the Edward Robinson Professor of Biblical Theology in 1890, and during his inaugural lecture, given 20 January 1891, he addressed the question of biblical inspiration. Briggs attacked the Princeton penchant for rationalistic defenses of the Bible as ''bibliolatry.'' He dismissed the notion of verbal inspiration, that the Holy Spirit had inspired every word of the Bible, and he allowed that the Scriptures contained errors that simply could not be explained away.[24]

Such ''progressive'' views caused Briggs considerable trouble with more conservative Presbyterians. At its meeting in 1891 the General Assembly exercised its prerogative and vetoed Briggs's appointment to the Robinson chair at Union. On 4 November 1891 Briggs was brought to trial by the Presbytery of New York on charges of heresy. He skillfully defended himself before standing-room-only crowds in New York's Scotch Presbyterian Church, and the case was dismissed. A year later, however, Briggs was tried a second time, a five-week ordeal that attracted national media attention. Once again he was acquitted. Undeterred, the General Assembly voted to try the case a third time. The trial, which opened on 29 May 1893 at the New York Avenue Church, this time ended in a conviction, and Brigg's Presbyterian ordination was suspended.

The quest for doctrinal purity on the matter of biblical inspiration, however, came at a price. Briggs himself remained a suspended Presbyterian until 1898 when he resigned his ordination; he was ordained an Episcopal priest the following year. The faculty and administration of Union had steadfastly supported Briggs throughout his sundry trials. In 1904 Union finally severed all official ties with Presbyterianism and became an independent institution. The board no longer required subscription to the Westminster standards or endorsement of presbyterian polity.

As the nineteenth century drew to a close, northern Presbyterians could look back on a period of radical change that had dramatically reshaped their denomination. With the formation of Princeton Theological Seminary, various other seminaries, and numerous colleges around the country, Presbyterians easily kept pace with their countrymen in an era of institution building, but successive schisms—over revivalism, slavery, and biblical inspiration—shook and finally cracked the very foundations upon which those institutions were constructed. The Old School–New School schism festered for decades and contributed to other disputes. The sectional division lasted well over a century. And the doctrinal skirmishes between the liberals at Union Seminary and the conservative stalwarts at Princeton Seminary prefigured the fundamentalist–modernist controversy of the twentieth century.

NOTES

1. Philip Schaff, *America: A Sketch of Its Political, Social, and Religious Character*, ed. Perry Miller (Cambridge, Mass.: Harvard University Press, 1961), p. 118.

2. For a detailed treatment of the Cumberland revival and Presbyterianism in the South, see the following chapter.

3. Charles G. Finney, *Lectures on Revivals of Religion*, ed. William McLoughlin (Cambridge, Mass.: Harvard University Press, 1960), p. 13.

4. On the Rochester revival, particularly its utility for social control and enforcing middle-class values, see Paul E. Johnson, *A Shopkeeper's Millennium: Society and Revivals in Rochester, New York, 1815–1837* (New York: Hill & Wang, 1978).

5. Ibid., p. 269.

6. For an excellent treatment of the New School–Old School schism, see George M. Marsden, *The Evangelical Mind and the New School Presbyterian Experience: A Case Study of Thought and Theology in Nineteenth-Century America* (New Haven, Conn.: Yale University Press, 1970), chap. 3; see also Harold M. Parker, Jr., *The United Synod of the South: The Southern New School Presbyterian Church* (Westport, Conn.: Greenwood Press, 1988), chap. 1.

7. Quoted in Lefferts A. Loetscher, *A Brief History of the Presbyterians*, 3d ed. (Philadelphia: Westminster Press, 1978), p. 97.

8. This scene is suggested in a sketch, ca. 1817, by a visiting French artist, Charles-Alexandre Lesueur, at the Musée d'Histoire Naturelle, Le Havre. A reproduction appears on the dust jacket of George M. Marsden, *The Evangelical Mind and the New School Presbyterian Experience: A Case Study of Thought and Theology in Nineteenth-Century America* (New Haven, Conn.: Yale University Press, 1970).

9. Quoted in Mark A. Noll, ed., *The Princeton Theology, 1812–1921: Scripture, Science, and Theological Method from Archibald Alexander to Benjamin Breckinridge Warfield* (Grand Rapids, Mich.: Baker Book House, 1983), pp. 53, 54. Much of the information on the formation of Princeton Seminary comes from Mark A. Noll, "The Founding of Princeton Seminary," *Westminster Theological Journal* 42 (Fall 1979), 72–110.

10. On Witherspoon's influence and legacy, see the excellent discussion in Mark A. Noll, *Princeton and the Republic, 1768–1822* (Princeton, N.J.: Princeton University Press, 1989), chap. 4; on the percentage of graduates entering the ministry, see ibid., p. 53.

11. Quoted in Noll, ed., *Princeton Theology*, pp. 56, 57.

12. Quoted in Thomas Jefferson Wertenbaker, *Princeton 1746–1896* (Princeton, N.J.: Princeton University Press, 1946), p. 148.

13. Quoted in Noll, "Founding of Princeton Seminary," p. 97.

14. Quoted in ibid.

15. *Proceedings Connected with the Semi-Centennial Commemoration of the Professorship of Rev. Charles Hodge, D.D., LL.D in the Theological Seminary at Princeton, N.J., April 24, 1872* (New York: Anson D. F. Randolph & Co., n.d.), p. 52.

16. *The Centennial Celebration of the Theological Seminary of the Presbyterian Church in the United States of America at Princeton, New Jersey* (Princeton: Princeton Theological Seminary, 1912), p. 350.

17. On the *Princeton Review*, see Charles H. Lippy, s.v. *"The Princeton Review"* in *Religious Periodicals of the United States: Academic and Scholarly Journals*, ed. Charles H. Lippy (Westport, Conn.: Greenwood Press, 1986).

18. This account of the formation of Union Theological Seminary relies on Robert T. Handy, "Union Theological Seminary in New York and American Presbyterianism, 1836–1904," *American Presbyterians: Journal of Presbyterian History* 66 (Summer 1988), 115–122.

19. Quoted in ibid., p. 116.

20. See the following chapter.

21. Noll, ed., *Princeton Theology*, pp. 145–152; Jon H. Roberts, *Darwinism and the Divine in America: Protestant Intellectuals and Organic Evolution, 1859–1900* (Madison: University of Wisconsin Press, 1988), pp. 17–18.

22. Alexander to Mrs. Phebe Robinson, 16 February 1846, ms. at Princeton Theological Seminary.

23. See Randall Balmer, "Princetonians and Scripture: A Reconsideration," *Westminster Theological Journal* 44 (1982):352–365.

24. Regarding the Briggs case, see Robert T. Handy, *A History of Union Theological Seminary in New York* (New York: Columbia University Press, 1987), esp. chap. 4.

4
SOUTHERN PRESBYTERIANISM IN THE NINETEENTH CENTURY

Shortly after 1900, following a century that had seen American Presbyterianism divide over issues as diverse as revivalism, slavery, and biblical inerrancy, the General Assembly of the Presbyterian Church in the United States of America began consideration of a proposal that represented a remarkable opportunity for the church to adjust its position on several important issues. In 1904, committees from the Presbyterian Church in the United States of America, the historic "Northern Presbyterian Church," formalized merger negotiations with the Cumberland Presbyterian Church, formed in 1810 by revivalist ministers who withdrew from the Presbyterian Church over irreconcilable doctrinal and polity differences. Early in 1904 the committees charged with the negotiations submitted their Joint Report on Union to the respective denominations for action on or before 30 April 1905.

The proposed merger was of historic importance for several reasons, not least of which was that it would reunite two Presbyterian bodies that had been separated for nearly a century. Apart from the obvious significance of this denominational rapprochement, however, the merger became a forum for discussion of the issues that had been hotly contested within Presbyterian circles throughout the nineteenth century: revivalism, sectionalism, race relations, and the modernization of Calvinist orthodoxy. Spirited debates about these issues were largely responsible for changing the shape of Presbyterianism, especially in the American South. What had been a single denomination in 1800 had been divided, by the opening of the twentieth century, into three major Presbyterian bodies: the Presbyterian Church in the United States of America (located primarily in the North), the Presbyterian Church in the United States (located in the South), and the Cumberland Presbyterian Church (the body born of the Second Awakening in the Old Southwest). A number of social, political, and theological factors gave Presbyterianism in the nineteenth-century South its unique character.

THE LEGACY OF THE FRONTIER REVIVALS

As noted previously, the legitimacy of the Awakenings and revivals of the eighteenth and nineteenth centuries was contested among Presbyterians. During the Great Awakening of the late 1730s and early 1740s, Presbyterians had temporarily divided (in 1741) into two factions over the Awakening. New Side Presbyterians (like New Light Congregationalists in New England) welcomed the Awakening as the work of God; Old Side Presbyterians (whose sympathies ran parallel to the Old Lights among the Congregationalists) viewed both the theological defense and the emotional excesses of the Awakening with suspicion. Although the New Side and Old Side parties were reunited in 1758, the Presbyterian tradition suffered another, more substantive split in 1837. In great measure this nineteenth-century division of the Church into New School and Old School factions also stemmed from contrary assessments of religious revivals. The New School party, under the leadership of Lyman Beecher,* Albert Barnes,* and Henry Boynton Smith,* affirmed the revival tactics of the so-called Second Awakening that swept areas of Connecticut, upstate New York, and western frontier areas in Kentucky and Tennessee. Old School Presbyterians, notably Charles Hodge* of Princeton Seminary, on the other hand, resisted the progressive theology and innovative revival tactics of New School evangelists.[1] The battles between the New School and Old School parties were complex, and were particularly exacerbated by the sectional disputes that ultimately led to the Civil War. But the debates over the theological legitimacy of the revivals—particularly as they transpired in the West—had other lasting effects on American Presbyterianism.

James McGready,* the first and certainly the best-known Presbyterian revivalist of the nineteenth century, was reared in North Carolina by Scots-Irish parents. He experienced a religious conversion in 1786, after which he was ordained by the Redstone Presbytery for ministry in Stony Creek, North Carolina. Using techniques he had learned under the tutelage of John Blair Smith of Hampden—Sydney College, McGready quickly established a reputation as an aggressive revivalist. Resistance from antirevivalist opponents, however, forced McGready to relocate; in 1796 he accepted a call to serve three congregations—Gasper River, Red River, and Muddy River—in Logan County, Kentucky.

Within a year of his arrival, McGready and scores of other Presbyterian ministers (notable among them Barton Stone,* whose independent "Stoneite" group left the Presbyterian fold in 1804 and later became a constituent of Alexander Campbell's "Christian" denomination in 1832) found themselves at the helm of one of America's most unusual spiritual awakenings. These frontier revivals stretched across the Old Southwest region, and were particularly strong in Kentucky and Tennessee, culminating in the famous Cane Ridge meeting in August 1801.

As one prominent historian has noted, the Cane Ridge meeting "has challenged the descriptive powers of many historians, yet none has risen fully to the occasion.''[2] An enormous gathering—contemporary observers estimated the crowd of participants to have numbered between ten and twenty-five thousand—Cane Ridge was characterized by emotional excess, ecumenical inclusivity (Baptists and Methodists shared the leadership with McGready and his Presbyterian colleagues), and a series of the most curious physical manifestations ever to occur in American religion. Participants fell to the ground unconscious, sang and laughed spontaneously, danced uncontrollably, and emitted strange guttural sounds. These latter "exercises," known to skeptics as the "jerks" and the "barks," respectively, appear to have no parallel in American religious experience. Given its size, its duration (the meeting lasted four days), and its notoriety, the Cane Ridge meeting soon became the archetypal American frontier camp meeting revival—an effective ritual technique still employed in many American denominations.[3]

In the wake of frontier revivals such as Cane Ridge, and in the face of the growing need for clergy on the western frontier, Presbyterian ministers, like their colleagues in the Baptist and Methodist traditions, began to sanction the use of exhorters, who were trained and deployed to promote revivals. They preached extempore and literally "exhorted" those outside the churches to repent, confess their sins, and become members of local congregations. The prominence of exhorters in the western presbyteries became a contested issue among more traditional Presbyterians, however. Opponents objected to the fact that many exhorters lacked either university training or formal theological education. Supporters, on the other hand, noted that the Scottish church had made provision for the office, and that the American church's form of government did allow for exceptions to the normal requirement that candidates for the ministry hold at least a bachelor's degree.

In the fall of 1802 the Presbyterian Church organized the Synod of Kentucky. As part of this restructuring, the synod divided Transylvania Presbytery, where the debate about the use of exhorters had been particularly acrimonious, into two separate presbyteries: Transylvania and Cumberland. From the outset, ministers in the Cumberland Presbytery were equally divided; five were committed revivalists, and five were either unwilling to sanction the revivals or were directly opposed to them. This precarious balance of power, however, did not last long. At the first meeting of the Cumberland Presbytery in April 1803, the presbytery received into membership John Haw, who had recently been recognized by the Transylvania Presbytery. Haw's presence gave the prorevival party a majority in the presbytery, an advantage upon which they soon capitalized. Within a year the ranks of the prorevival faction swelled considerably; on any issue before the presbytery they could easily marshal the support of a majority of the voting presbyters.[4]

The antirevival party, despite its minority status in the councils of the Cumberland Presbytery, continued to make itself felt. When the revival faction proposed the addition of even more exhorters to the ranks of the presbytery, the antirevivalists took offense. David Rice,* of the revivalist party of the Tran-

sylvania Presbytery, asked the General Assembly for advice on the use of exhorters. In response to Rice's query the Assembly of 1804 upheld the office of
exhorter, but surrounded their affirmation with several caveats. Exhorters were
not to be considered standing officers in the presbytery, they were to be appointed and removed at the discretion of the presbytery, and they were expected to obtain
an education, after which they could apply for regular ordination.

Although the antirevivalists were a minority in Cumberland Presbytery, their
party held a majority in the Transylvania Presbytery and in the Synod of Kentucky
as well. Wary of the power the revivalists were amassing in the Cumberland
Presbytery, and interpreting the Assembly's caveats about the role of exhorters
as support for their position, the antirevivalist party pressed their case before
the synod. Though the synod deferred action for at least a year, it eventually
chose a special commission of examination before which several newly elected
exhorters were required to appear. Several Cumberland ministers, including
McGready, Samuel McAdow,* and William Hodge, objected to the proceedings,
arguing that the commission was usurping the constitutional rights of the presbytery to ordain whomever it saw fit.

But these objections proved to be of little consequence. In December 1805,
the commission, with full synodical powers, prohibited five ordained ministers,
six probationers, and fifteen exhorters—all young men recently recognized in
the Cumberland Presbytery—from further ministerial activity. Having dealt with
the younger members of Cumberland Presbytery, the commission then required
three older revivalist Cumberland ministers, William Hodge, William McGee,
and John Rankin, to appear before the next meeting of the synod to defend
themselves against the charge of holding doctrines contrary to the Confession
of Faith. In 1806 Hodge and Rankin appeared before a synod committee organized for the purpose of examining the charges of heresy against them. Although
they were cleared of the charges, these two revivalists remained steadfast in their
refusal to request their Cumberland Presbytery colleagues to appear before the
synod commission for examination. For their recalcitrance, the two were suspended from the ministry by the synod, and in a final blow to the revival party,
the synod dissolved the Cumberland Presbytery and assigned its members to the
Transylvania Presbytery.[5]

Although the controversy continued for nearly four years, with appeals, proposals, and letters of counsel moving freely between Cumberland presbyters,
Transylvania Presbytery, and Synod of Kentucky, and the General Assembly,
the complaints of the revival party—now cast in the role of a dissenting group—
went unanswered. On 4 February 1810, leaders of this group met in Dixon
County, Tennessee, to take definitive action. Samuel McAdow, Finis Ewing,*
and Samuel King formed an independent presbytery, aptly named the Cumberland Presbytery. The following month, at its first official gathering, the body
numbered four ministers (McAdow, Ewing, King, and Ephriam McLean), five
licentiates, and six candidates for the ministry.

Although the Cumberland Church was born out of the judicial struggles directly stemming from the exhorter controversy, a doctrinal debate that had been a part of the larger New School–Old School dispute was also a factor in the formation of the new body. In the statement in which McAdow, Ewing, and King had declared themselves independent, they adopted the "confession and discipline of the Presbyterian church," but with one caveat: They rejected "the idea of fatality, that seems to be taught under the mysterious doctrine of predestination."[6] This refusal to adopt one of the chief tenets of Calvinism, one particularly conspicuous in the Westminster Confession, greatly affected the Cumberland Presbyterians' subsequent attempts at reconciliation with the larger Presbyterian Church. Indeed, up until 1813 the Cumberland group held conversations with representatives of other presbyteries, all aimed at rapprochement. But the Cumberland withdrawal was ultimately finalized not on revival or judicial matters, but on theological grounds. The parent body, as it had for nearly a century, required all ministers fully to affirm the Westminster Confession. The Cumberland group, however, continued to insist that Westminster's predestinarian platform taught a dubious "fatalism" that was inimical to revivals. This point of contention remained unresolved, and near the end of 1812 other presbyteries of the parent body, chief among them the Presbytery of West Tennessee, broke communion with the Cumberland group.

Due perhaps to the publicity generated by the lengthy controversy, the maverick Cumberland body had posted substantial growth during the three years following its formation as an independent presbytery in 1810. In the spring of 1813, after it became certain that there would be no amicable reunion, the Cumberland Presbytery met in Sumner County, Tennessee, and formed the Cumberland Synod, made up of three presbyteries: Logan, Cumberland, and Elk. At the first formal meeting of the new synod in October 1813 the new body—soon to be named the Cumberland Presbyterian Church—drew up a formal constitution. It adopted the Westminster Confession with four exceptions: First, it rejected the idea that some people were eternally reprobate before God; second, it rejected the limited atonement; third, it rejected the doctrine of infant damnation, and in its place affirmed the doctrine that infants who died were saved by Christ; and fourth, in a derivative point stemming from its rejection of the limited atonement, it noted that God's Spirit operated on humanity in such a way as to leave all people without excuse for their sins.[7]

The Cumberland Presbyterian Church, a denomination positioned in the "border states" region of the nation during the Civil War, continued its independent existence for nearly a century. Its unique situation—geographically perched between North and South, and theologically placed between traditional Presbyterian orthodoxy and frontier, Arminian revivalism—made the Cumberland Church a distinctly American hybrid within the Presbyterian tradition. Until 1906, when a large portion of the Cumberland Church merged with the Presbyterian Church in the U.S.A., the Cumberland body carried on its unique traditions of aggressive evangelism in America's mid-South.

THE SECTIONAL CRISIS

During the 1830s tensions between the major Presbyterian parties in the United States, the Old School and the New School, exacerbated. The Old School, led by Charles Hodge of Princeton Theological Seminary, hardened its opposition to the progressive Plan of Union of 1801, under which Presbyterians and New England Congregationalists became allied. The Plan, Hodge argued, subverted traditional Presbyterian polity and effectively placed "Union" churches, as well as several powerful missions organizations, outside church control. Moreover, Old Schoolers took offense at the liberalized Calvinism of New School theologians such as Lyman Beecher, Albert Barnes, and Henry Boynton Smith. New School advocates, on the other hand, believed that church union, based on a broader, more inclusive version of the Reformed tradition, and inspired by the progressive Calvinism that influenced both revivalism and social reform, represented the most promising course for both Presbyterians and Congregationalists in a rapidly changing nineteenth-century America.

Distinctly theological matters differentiated the two schools, but the preeminent national political issues of the era—the sectional crisis between North and South, and the ongoing debate about slavery—also affected the growing tensions between Presbyterianism's major factions. As the schools contended for power in the denomination at large, sectional demographic differences became increasingly pronounced. The traditional strongholds of American Presbyterianism lay in what would become the Union states during the Civil War; hence, both the Old School and the New School found their greatest strengths in the North. The Presbyterian churches of the South were represented in both Schools, however: Southerners constituted about an eighth of the New School churches and little more than a third of the Old School congregations.[8]

Beginning in 1835 Old School partisans began to circulate a document called the "Act and Testimony," which laid out their concerns about the progressive theology of the New School. By the General Assembly of 1837 the theological debate between the parties festered into a schism. Old Schoolers, who held a clear majority in the 1837 Assembly, successfully moved to have the 1801 Plan of Union declared unconstitutional. To boos and hisses from the floor of the Assembly, the Old School, led by two powerful Virginians, George Baxter and William S. Plumer, officially removed four synods from the church—all of these in the North: Western Reserve, Geneva, Utica, and Genessee—which had been created under the Plan. This action, by which the Old School cast off over five hundred churches with a combined membership of over one hundred thousand, effectively set the stage for the formal bifurcation of the American Presbyterian tradition. Within a year of the 1837 debacle, both New School and Old School groups organized separate General Assemblies. The Presbyterian Church (Old School) found its greatest strength in the mid-Atlantic states, particularly in New Jersey and eastern Pennsylvania. The New School, which held nearly half of the original membership of the denomination, was most strongly represented in New York.

As the sectional crisis mounted, both Old School and New School bodies were forced to attend to the issue of slavery. The New School, despite its heritage of social reform, had managed to avoid confrontations about the issue of slavery for nearly two decades. Delegates to the New School Assembly of 1850, however, many of them ardent abolitionists, affirmed a document in clear opposition to slavery: "We exceedingly deplore the working of the whole system of slavery . . . as fraught with many and great evils to the civil, political and moral interests of those regions where it exists."[9] At the 1853 Assembly the church directed its presbyteries to report on the progress each had made to eliminate the evil of slavery. Predictably, Southern New School elders objected to both the 1850 statement and the subsequent call for reform. Their first line of defense, a rhetorical move typical of many Southern Protestants, was based on the Scriptures. Arguing that the Bible never proscribed slaveholding, these apologists believed that the South, if left to solve the problem on its own, would eventually surmount the problem of slavery. Northern New Schoolers, however, took little solace in this prediction.

In the 1855 New School Assembly, the abolitionist party of the church took an action that boded ill for the Southern contingent of the church; they appointed a committee to research the constitutional rules that would govern any disciplinary action the Assembly might take against slaveholding members or against recalcitrant presbyteries in which slavery was condoned. During the very months in which the special committee considered what judicial options the church might exercise, however, the secular courts took similar matters under consideration. In March 1857, just two days after the inauguration of President James Buchanan, the United States Supreme Court published its famous *Dred Scott* judgment. That decision, which declared that Negro slaves were not to be considered citizens and, hence, had no civil recourse in federal courts, encouraged Southern slaveholders at the very moment when the New School Assembly appeared to be preparing to discipline them. Buoyed by the *Dred Scott* decision, the Presbytery of Lexington defended its slaveholding members by appealing to the Scriptures, thereby defying the church's call for reform. In a rapid series of apparently inevitable events, the New School church was rent along sectional lines. The General Assembly censured Lexington Presbytery for its recalcitrance. Soon after, however, Lexington garnered the support of several Southern synods. This group withdrew from the Assembly in 1857, and formed the United Synod of the Presbyterian Church in the U.S.A. in 1858. Some Southern New School presbyteries resisted the formation of the new body; indeed, some chose to reunite with the Old School church. These defections notwithstanding, by 1861 the United Synod maintained three synods, comprised of thirteen presbyteries, about two hundred congregations, and over ten thousand members.[10]

The sectional crisis, fueled by the debate about slavery, had rent the New

School church, and so would it divide the Presbyterian Church, Old School. This is not to suggest, however, that the Old School had not already experienced tensions that broke out along sectional lines. Since the 1837 New School–Old School schism, several Southern Old School clergy, notably Robert L. Dabney,* Robert J. Breckinridge,* Benjamin Morgan Palmer,* and James Henley Thornwell,* had helped to develop a distinctly Southern version of Old School polity. Several theological issues had served to focus North–South theological tensions in the Old School; three of the most important among them were the rights and responsibilities of ruling elders in the church, the power of church boards, and, most important, the ''spirituality'' of the church. On each of these questions Thornwell, chief spokesman for Southern Old School Presbyterians, developed and defended a distinctly Southern view; his Northern Old School counterpart in debate was Charles Hodge of Princeton Seminary.

Traditional Presbyterian polity affirmed a system of ordination that differentiated between two types of elders. Teaching elders functioned as the clergy; they were often university trained and attended to a wide range of pastoral duties such as preaching, teaching, and administering the sacraments. In distinction to the teaching elder, however, Presbyterian polity also recognized ruling elders; these leaders had no special theological training but held positions on local sessions and aided in the sacramental ministry of the congregation. Both types of elders participated at the presbytery, synod, and General Assembly levels of church government. During the early 1840s a debate about the authority of ruling elders arose in the Old School.[11] Hodge, representing the Northern position, sought to circumscribe the authority of a ruling elder; he maintained that their presence at presbytery meetings should not count toward a quorum and that they should not participate in the ordination of teaching elders by the ''laying on of hands.'' Although the Assembly of 1843 adopted Hodge's position on these matters, Thornwell and Breckinridge were vociferous in their opposition to the decision. They argued that the Scriptures were clear on the matter; traditional Presbyterian polity and doctrine was clear and unalterable, for it had been instituted by divine law. Though these Southern apologists were outmaneuvered in the initial debates about the matter, their position came to characterize Southern Presbyterian polity.

The relationship of denominational boards and voluntary societies had been a chief point of contention during the Old School–New School debates that led to the schism of 1837. Although the Old School church had tightened control of the boards, several Southerners believed that these reforms had not gone far enough. Breckinridge and Thornwell mounted a two-pronged case against the existing Old School boards. They maintained that the size of the boards was far too large (in 1840, for instance, the Board of Foreign Missions had 120 members) and that life memberships were granted to many individuals on the basis of financial support they had rendered to the work of the various boards on which they served. Thornwell attacked the system in more fundamental ways as well; as he understood the matter, the church was unwise to trust the governance of these particular ministries of the church at large to a small representative group. Control of the boards properly belonged to either the presbyteries or the General Assembly. At the Old School Assembly of 1860, the debate was formally joined. Again, the debate found Thornwell pitted against Hodge, and again each of these prominent theologians appealed to the authority of the Bible. Hodge and the Northern contingent argued that the governing structures of the church were permitted to adopt any practice not proscribed by Scripture. Thornwell, on the other hand, took a more conservative position, and asserted that the Church could only practice that which Scripture positively commanded. The Assembly adopted the Northern rationale, ruling that the boards were free to act as they saw fit. The Assembly counseled only smaller reforms; the boards were directed to abolish life memberships and to become more fully accountable to the Assembly. Again, Thornwell and the Southern Old School apologists tasted defeat.[12]

Although the debates about elders and the boards concerned matters essentially judicial, the theological problem that increasingly divided the Old School along sectional lines was the notion of the "spirituality" of the church. This debate, more than any other, would underlie what became the most explosive controversy of the era—the problem of slavery. In the decades following the schism of 1837, Presbyterian theologians attended to a theological problem of great antiquity among Christians, namely, the issue of church's role in culture at large and, particularly, its relationship to civil authority. As early as 1847 Old School leaders had debated this issue in reference to public education. As the denomination sought to extend its influence into culture at large, the notion of Presbyterian parochial education became popular. Increasingly, presbyteries and synods sponsored academies, colleges, and theological seminaries expressly intended to promote the education of Presbyterians. Apart from the boon this development represented to Presbyterian denominational growth, advocates argued that its other important contribution would be to afford the church an opportunity to promote a distinctly Christian worldview to the populace at large.

Some Presbyterian theorists, Thornwell and Breckinridge among them, opposed this notion of Presbyterian education, however. They believed that the state, and not the church, should take responsibility for educating the citizenry, and they based this conclusion on the doctrine of the spirituality of the church. The mission of the church, they maintained, was purely spiritual; its purpose and, hence, its jurisdiction, extended only to matters of religious faith. After considerable debate in the popular religious press and in several ecclesiastical judicatures, the Old School General Assembly adopted a modified plan of parochial education for children ages five through twelve. Once again, however, the movement had its greatest strength in the Northern presbyteries of the Old School Church; Presbyterian parochial schools in the South were few in number and, with the onset of the Civil War, most of these institutions closed their doors.

These Southern losses in the theological struggles within the Old School church augured even more ominous developments. Despite internal theological differences, the gathering political controversies of the sectional crisis, and the ecclesiastical schisms that followed in its wake, the Old School church had managed to remain united despite its sectional differences. As the sectional crisis grew during the 1850s so did Southern fears that the North, led by uncompromising abolitionists, would usurp their rights as sovereign states.

In this highly charged atmosphere Thornwell in 1850 launched a campaign in defense of the Southern church's autonomy, employing precisely the same argument he had used to oppose the parochial school plan. In the face of increasing Northern hostility to the notion that Christians could own slaves, Thornwell not only defended the practice as being permitted by Scripture, but he also aggressively disputed the notion that the church had the right to address the question of slavery—a civil matter, he judged—much less adopt an authoritative position on the matter. With the election of Abraham Lincoln in 1860 Southern Old Schoolers echoed the rhetoric of political and ecclesial secessionists (in addition to the New School division of 1861, the national Baptist and Methodist bodies had divided along sectional lines in 1845[13]) and began to call for the formation of a separate Southern Old School Presbyterian denomination. Although some Southern Old School ministers counseled caution in this matter, notably R. L. Dabney and other faculty members at Union Theological Seminary in Virginia, Thornwell and Palmer led the campaign for withdrawal.

As the Union itself was sundered by the seccession of several Southern states, so too ecclesiastical union began to fracture. After considerable debate at the Old School General Assembly, begun 16 May 1861 in Philadelphia, the Assembly passed a resolution written by Gardiner Spring,* pastor of the Brick Church in New York City. The resolution, adopted over the protest of Charles Hodge and others who believed that it represented the church's formal entry into matters properly left to the state, forthrightly affirmed the church's support of the federal Union. Within three months disgruntled Southern Old Schoolers gathered in Atlanta and planned for the formation of a separate Southern Old School denomination.

In December 1861 this group held its first General Assembly in Augusta, Georgia. Thornwell, who had ably served as the Southern Old School's most persuasive apologist, became the chief architect of the separation. Although he was not nominated for the position of moderator due to his failing health (Palmer was elected to that position), Thornwell was active on the floor of the Assembly. On his motion the body adopted the rules and confessional standards of the Old School and then took the name The Presbyterian Church in the Confederate States of America. Thornwell's greatest contribution to the Assembly, and perhaps to the Southern church as a whole, came in the closing days of the gathering.

Considerably weakened by the illness that would claim his life within a year, Thornwell rose and delivered an ''Address by the General Assembly to the Churches of Jesus Christ throughout the Earth.'' Although the address had been prepared under the auspices of a representative committee chosen on the second day of the Assembly, it was common knowledge that Thornwell was its chief author. In his soliloquy he attended to several urgent matters.[14] Thornwell admonished his auditors not to judge the separation of the Old School into two regional bodies as a schism. Rather, the separation was intended for the peace of the churches and dedicated to the glory of God. Thornwell adduced three reasons in support of the separation. First, he returned to the theme of the "spirituality of the church" and argued that the Old School Assembly of 1861, by its partisan affirmation of the federal Union, had grievously usurped authority that properly belonged only to the state. This action, Thornwell argued, opened the door to "the worst passions of human nature, into the deliberations of Church Courts."[15] Had Southerners acquiesced in this error, he noted, the spiritual purity of the church would be forever tarnished by worldly politics. Second, Thornwell defended the notion that churches were best organized along national lines. The Confederacy was to be considered one among the nations of the world, and it was only proper that it have its own unique national denominations. Third, Thornwell took up the issue of slavery. At the start, he admitted that this issue was chief among the difficulties that separated North and South. The central issue for Thornwell was the position churches took in regard to the institution of slavery. He noted that the new church—in its ecclesiastical role—held no distinct position on the slavery question: "In our ecclesiastical capacity, we are neither the friends nor the foes of slavery . . . we have no commission either to propogate it or abolish it. The policy of its existence or non-existence is a question which exclusively belongs to the State. We have no right, as a Church, to enjoin it as a duty, or to condemn it as a sin."[16] Given this platform, Thornwell affirmed the positive benefits of slavery. The black race, he believed, stood lower than the white race on the "scale of being." This being so, as long as the black race "coexists, side by side, with the white [race], bondage is its normal condition." Slavery, a "kindly and benevolent" system, could help to elevate the African slaves; benevolent masters could rescue the slaves from barbarism and sin.[17] Thornwell's address was well-received by the Assembly; in a closing ceremony, all present affixed their signatures to the document.

By the opening of the Civil War, then, the Confederate states had two distinctively Southern Presbyterian denominations—a smaller, New School body (the United Synod of the Presbyterian Church in the U.S.A.) and the larger Old School body (The Presbyterian Church in the Confederate States of America). Throughout the War, both denominations defended the Southern cause. Hundreds of parish ministers left their congregational duties, especially during the summer months, and enlisted as chaplains in the Confederate Army. They preached to enormous gatherings of soldiers, attended to the wounded and dying, and in some cases led successful religious revivals.

Although many Southerners had been confident that the war would be short, the realities of America's most deadly conflict soon shattered their optimism. Confederate losses in the field mounted, and at home many local congregations witnessed the decimation of their membership to conscription and military casualties, succumbed to horrible poverty, and, in many cases, suffered the physical destruction of church property. By 1864, despite the optimistic accounts published by the popular press, and notwithstanding innumerable patriotic sermons delivered by Confederate ministers, the outcome of the War seemed evident even to the staunchest Southern apologists—the South would soon be defeated.

During 1864, however, there was at least one cause for celebration among Southern Presbyterians. In previous months R. L. Dabney had been appointed to chair a committee to confer with representatives of the United Synod about a possible merger of the two Southern Presbyterian bodies. At the 1864 Assembly of the Presbyterian Church in the Confederate States of America, Dabney's committee recommended that the bodies unite. After four days of strenuous debate, the Assembly voted to adopt the recommendations of the committee, despite the resistance of Palmer and several other powerful conservatives. The United Synod ratified the plan in its next meeting, though several presbyteries, especially those in Tennessee, were prevented by the war from sending representatives to participate in the Union vote. This series of negotiations resulted in the formation of one of America's most important ecclesiastical bodies, the Presbyterian Church in the United States.

NORTHERN PRESBYTERIANISM AND RACIAL ISSUES

Although the close of the Civil War brought a formal end to the sectional crisis and to the institution of slavery in the United States, Presbyterians in both the North and the South were forced to confront the challenges posed by the rapid emancipation of millions of African-Americans. In the antebellum North Presbyterians had successfully formed several congregations of free blacks. In 1807 Archibald Alexander* formed the Presbyterian Evangelical Society of Philadelphia, a group committed to the growth of Presbyterianism by means of aggressive evangelism. With Alexander's enthusiastic support, and under the leadership of John Gloucester (former slave of Gideon Blackburn,* the Presbyterian "apostle" to the Cherokees), the First African Presbyterian Church began in 1807 with twenty-two members. In 1811, the year in which the congregation received official recognition from the presbytery, the congregation had grown to include 122 members.[18] All of Gloucester's three sons became Presbyterian ministers. Jeremiah Gloucester succeeded his father at First African in 1824. Subsequently, the congregation was rent by several controversies, two of which were responsible for the formation of additional black Presbyterian congregations in Philadelphia: the Second African Presbyterian Church, founded in 1824, and Lombard Street Central Church, under the ministerial leadership of another son of John Gloucester, Stephen. Other Northern cities also became sites for black Presbyterian congregations. Congregations were established in New York City (1822), Reading, Pennsylvania (1823), Newark, New Jersey (1835), the District of Columbia (1841), Princeton, New Jersey (1845), Baltimore, Maryland (1853), and Harrisburg, Pennsylvania (1858). These churches were under the able leadership of a cadre of African-American Presbyterian ministers: Elymas P. Rogers, a free black from Connecticut who was licensed by the Old

School Presbytery of New Brunswick in 1844; Samuel Cornish,* free-born black who became the first ordained minister of the First Colored Presbyterian Church in New York City; ex-slave J.W.C. Pennington, who served the First Colored Church in New York City from 1848 to 1856; Theodore S. Wright,* the first black graduate from a Presbyterian seminary (Princeton Theological Seminary in 1828).[19]

After the war, and in concert with other Reconstruction efforts to alleviate the enormous problems facing freed slaves, the Presbyterian Church in the United States of America dispatched missionaries, teachers, and other church workers to the South. Though few churches were begun by these Northern emissaries, they were quite successful in their educational efforts, Indeed, one historian argues that these educational endeavors represented Presbyterianism's most significant contributions to the black community.[20]

Northern Presbyterians, then, had developed strategies for including free Northern blacks in their denomination throughout the antebellum period. After Emancipation, however, such Northern Presbyterian overtures to blacks largely ceased. Historic black congregations increasingly sought ecclesial independence from the predominantly white—and increasingly segregationist—denomination. These losses notwithstanding, Northern Presbyterians shifted their attention to Reconstruction social programs designed to aid freed slaves in the South.

SOUTHERN PRESBYTERIANISM AND RACIAL ISSUES

The demise of the Confederacy did little to change Southerners' attitudes about their region of the country or about the social status of freed slaves in their midst. Nor were the problems of sectionalism and race relations limited to the civil realm; throughout the period of Reconstruction and well into the twentieth century Presbyterians who dwelt south of the Mason-Dixon line reflected the attitudes of their distinctive Southern ethos. Southern Presbyterian efforts among African-Americans changed with emancipation, but not in substantive ways. Until the war, Southern Presbyterians had been satisfied to work within the confines of the slave system; after emancipation, they acquiesced to the caste system of social segregation based on race.

Prior to the Civil War, Southern Presbyterian ministry to black slaves operated on an entirely different basis. Presbyterian converts among the slaves were not permitted to form independent congregations. Instead, they attended white Presbyterian churches but were generally barred from officeholding and were seated in separate areas of the sanctuary. The first Presbyterian missionary to slaves was a free black named John Chavis,* who was appointed a missionary by the 1801 General Assembly. Chavis began preaching to plantation slaves, although his audiences were often racially mixed. After Nat Turner's insurrection in 1831, however, Chavis and black ministers in other denominations found it increasingly difficult to hold preaching services for slaves; white fears of slave revolts led to a ban on blacks preaching to black audiences.

Perhaps the most prominent organizer of plantation missions was a white Presbyterian minister named Charles Colcock Jones.* Jones had long been interested in missions to the slaves. Beginning in 1833 he worked in Savannah, Georgia, for nearly two decades developing plantation missions in concert with the Association for the Religious Instruction of Negroes. Jones, himself a Southern planter, deplored the manner in which the churches had neglected missions to slaves, yet he also recognized that the missions operation had to be circumscribed by the slave system.[21]

Like Baptists and Methodists in the postwar South, both the Presbyterian Church in the United States and the Cumberland Presbyterian Church rapidly adopted systems of ecclesiastical segregation. Reeling from the loss of the Confederacy, Presbyterians in the South resisted the notion of giving freed slaves an independent ecclesial existence. Instead, they settled for a system in which there was no parity between white and black ministers (black ministers were not seated at presbytery meetings, for example) and in which black congregations were connected with (but subordinate to) white congregations.[22] The inequities of this system did not go entirely unchallenged, however. Within several decades of the war, black Presbyterians from both the Presbyterian Church in the United States and the Cumberland Presbyterian Church withdrew to form synods and denominations separate from white domination. In this respect black Presbyterians followed the lead of Richard Allen, the first African-American ordained to the ministry. Although Allen had sought to remain within the Methodist Church, the persistent segregation of the races and discrimination against black Methodists led Allen to form a black denomination, the African Methodist Episcopal Church, free of white influence and control.

In the Presbyterian Church in the United States, there were few historically black congregations. In the postwar South, black antipathies to Presbyterianism were evident in the growth of independent black denominations erected on Baptist and Methodist models. By the 1890s Southern Presbyterians could count only twenty-four black ministers and some seven hundred black members on their rolls. In 1901, under the leadership of A. L. Philips and E. W. Williams, both prominent leaders among black Presbyterians, an independent body, the Afro-American Presbyterian Synod, was formed. The synod had a brief and tenuous existence; it rejoined the Presbyterian Church in the United States in 1917, becoming a black—and segregated—synod called the Snedecor Memorial Synod. It was not until 1951 that the denomination integrated the churches of Snedecor Memorial Synod into its otherwise white synodical structure.[23]

Like other Southern churches, Cumberland Presbyterians had struggled to maintain neutrality on the matter of slavery—they would neither make slaveholding a duty nor proscribe it—and had resisted the dissolution of the Union. Due to these efforts the denomination barely avoided a sectional schism at the opening of the War. But in the postwar years the Cumberland Church was dominated by Southerners, and by 1868 it was evident that segregated parishes would become the norm.[24] There were sufficient numbers of black Cumberland members in 1871, however, to lead the church to form the "First Synod of the Colored Cumberland Presbyterian Church." Within two years the black Cumberland Presbyterians withdrew and formed their own denomination, alternately known as the Negro Cumberland Presbyterian Church or the Cumberland Presbyterian Church, Colored.

THE MODERNIZATION OF CALVINIST ORTHODOXY

In his authoritative *A Religious History of the American People*, Sydney Ahlstrom claimed that Charles Darwin's *The Origin of Species*, published in 1859, was "the most important book of the century."[25] Darwin was not the first to question literal readings of the Bible; Charles Lyell's influential *Principles of Geology*, published nearly twenty-five years before Darwin's treatise, had promulgated theories that—implicitly, at least—contradicted biblical creation accounts. The publication of Darwin's work, however, became the focal point of a heated science versus Scripture debate that would plague American Christianity for a century or more. Although many of the most celebrated Presbyterian skirmishes took place in Northern Presbyterian seminaries—particularly at Princeton and Union, New York—Southern institutions were not untouched by the controversy.

This is not to suggest, however, that either Northern or Southern Presbyterians were anti-intellectual or anti-scientific. Indeed, in 1860 Columbia Theological Seminary instituted the Perkins Professorship of Natural Science in Connection with Revelation. This chair, the first of its kind in an American school of divinity, was specifically intended to provide an opportunity for the Columbia faculty and student body to probe what were now the competing claims of the new science and the revealed truths of the Bible. Although many nineteenth-century Christians would ultimately find the claims of science and orthodoxy fundamentally irreconcilable (a conviction that would explode onto the American scene during the fundamentalist controversy of the twentieth century), many Presbyterian leaders in both the North and the South were convinced that believers could study and learn from the new science and remain faithful to the authority of the Scriptures.

This confidence was based on a particularly nuanced philosophical rationale given shape by the Scottish philosophers Thomas Reid and Dugald Stewart. Known in America as Scottish common sense realism, this system relied on the conviction that "basic truths are much the same for all persons in all times and places."[26] Unbiased and judicious inquirers, using their innate common sense and the canons of scientific inquiry developed by Sir Francis Bacon, could examine a proposition and discern its truth or falsity. This theory of knowledge was particularly important in the pursuit of divine truth, whether it be found in special revelation, the Scriptures, or in general revelation, the created order. Either of these sources, if honestly appraised by the Christian, would yield divine truth in abundance. Always identified by its advocates as being genuinely scientific, many nineteenth-century apologists employed common sense to defend traditional theology against the assaults of the German higher critics of the Bible and the "speculation" of modern scientists (or, as common sense thinkers would have it, "pseudo-scientists") such as Darwin and Lyell.

Due in large measure to the traditional Scottish influence on American Presbyterian thought, American theologians such as John Witherspoon,* Charles Hodge, James Henley Thornwell, and the first incumbent of the Perkins Chair, James Woodrow,* drank deeply from the well of common sense thought. Although the evolution controversy would generate an enormous debate among Old School and New School factions in the North, Southern Presbyterians—like their equally conservative Southern Baptist cousins—quickly squelched the evolution controversy. Only one major battle took place in the Southern Old School, and that centered on Woodrow's work at Columbia Seminary.

The establishment of the Perkins Chair in 1860 was hailed by many Southern Presbyterian clergy as an important development for the life of the church. Thornwell, one of the strongest supporters of the chair, was perhaps the South's leading common sense thinker. Thornwell had discovered the utility of the common sense system as an undergraduate, while trying to adjudicate the competing claims of two of his professors, Thomas Cooper, a deist and freethinker, and Robert Henry, who had schooled Thornwell in the canons of orthodox Calvinism. From Thornwell's perspective the Perkins Chair represented a marvelous platform from which the church could examine and then harmonize the apparently contradictory claims of science and Scripture.

Woodrow's appointment to the position appeared nearly perfect. Woodrow had received the finest scientific education, and he was committed to holding in dynamic tension the truths of science and Scripture. Throughout his career he maintained that these two sources of truth were only apparently contradictory. The Scriptures, he believed, did not conform to the scientific genre; nor were the speculations of the evolutionists and geologists capable of empirical demonstration. Hence, inquiring Christian intellectuals could learn from and affirm both of these bodies of reliable data provided that they understood the respective limits of each genre.

Despite the support of Thornwell and other influential common sense theologians, however, during the 1870s and 1880s Southerners expressed increasing resistance to the claims of modern science. Although Woodrow insisted that he had always considered the evolutionary theory of the origins of the human race to be a pernicious error, increasingly he was forced to defend his moderate, circumscribed affirmation of the new science against the rhetorical assaults of anti-evolution critics. Chief among Woodrow's antagonists was the Old School theologian Robert L. Dabney, who feared that the evolutionary theory would infect the church with skepticism and foster a virulent strain of anti-Christian naturalism. Dabney published a series of essays that were sharply critical of the new science. Although Woodrow had sought to avoid open controversy, he found himself unable to remain silent in the face of these attacks. In an essay titled "An Examination of Certain Recent Assaults on Physical Science" published in July 1873, Woodrow defended scientific inquiry against Dabney, who, in Woodrow's estimation, had spoken as one who was ignorant of the true goals of scientific inquiry.

Dabney, of course, did not suffer the rebuke in silence; both in a published response and in the pulpit, he argued that human science must always defer to the revealed truths of the Bible. In a second essay, "A Further Examination of Certain Recent Assaults on Physical Science," published in 1874, and in an exchange of letters with Dabney, Woodrow isolated the point of contention that stood between them. Dabney, Woodrow claimed, insisted that the absence of supernatural force must be proven prior to using arguments about the causality operative in the natural order. For his part, Woodrow argued that a Christian scientist must first prove the presence of supernatural forces; then and only then could science be used in offering an account of the origins of the natural world.[27] The point of contention, then, rested on the matter of what presuppositions a Christian brought to the realm of scientific inquiry.

During the course of his ongoing debate with Dabney, Woodrow served as editor of the influential *Southern Presbyterian Review*. Soon after he had declared himself opposed to Dabney, rumors circulated about the doctrinal reliability of the *Review*; there were even suggestions that another journal, one more palatable to Dabney partisans, might be started. Although friends rallied to Woodrow's defense, the tide of public opinion began to turn against him. In 1884, at the insistence of Joseph Mack, a member of Columbia Seminary's governing board, the seminary called on Woodrow to give a full account of his views on evolution. This request, ostensibly intended to allay the mounting suspicions of Woodrow and the seminary, was Mack's first move in a carefully orchestrated campaign to oust Woodrow. In his statement delivered before Columbia's Alumni Association in May 1884 and subsequently published, Woodrow reminded his audience that Scripture and science were not mutually contradictory systems. The evolutionary theory, he maintained, gave no reliable or authoritative account of the creation of humankind. Woodrow observed that although God certainly had created the human soul immediately, the Creator might well have allowed organic life—including the human body—to develop naturally and mediately over time, through an evolutionary scheme. Although Woodrow's carefully nuanced alumni speech was received cordially, it was soon viewed as proof of his acceptance of Darwinism.

A public controversy soon arose. Although the seminary board, by a split vote, retained Woodrow on the faculty, the dissenters soon called for his ouster. Sensing a groundswell of popular opposition to Woodrow, now identified as an unflinching evolutionist, the board requested his resignation in December 1884. Woodrow refused to resign, preferring to have his case fully aired before the appropriate ecclesiastical courts. After more than a year of further wrangling within the church judicatures, his case was brought before the Assembly in 1886. The committee charged with examining the matter submitted a majority report that denied evolutionary theory in any form, for if evolution was accepted, they argued, then the inspiration of the Bible could not stand. Woodrow attempted without success to defend himself before the Assembly; subsequent appeals before several church courts also failed.

Despite his defeat, Woodrow's career continued. In 1894 he was recognized as a member of the South Carolina Presbytery, and he was elected moderator of the synod in 1901. He served as a professor, dean, and eventually president of South Carolina College, which would later become the University of South Carolina. These impressive achievements notwithstanding, however, Woodrow's careful appraisal of modern scientific theory, and his desire to maintain a distinctly Christian apologetic in an increasingly skeptical age, earned him infamy, not honor. His ouster strengthened the position of powerful traditionalists like Dabney and Mack, and ended any attempt to modernize the theology of Southern Presbyterianism from within.

FORGING A COALITION

The 1904 merger negotiations between the Presbyterian Church in the United States of America and the Cumberland Presbyterian Church, two major Presbyterian bodies, addressed all of the issues that had touched Presbyterian life in the nineteenth century. (The Presbyterian Church in the United States did not participate in the discussion.) After nearly a century of independent and largely successful existence, the Cumberland church expressed its willingness to rejoin the denomination from which it had withdrawn.

From the perspective of the Cumberland Presbyterians, several developments made merger attractive. In 1902 the Presbyterian Church U.S.A. had proposed several amendments to its Confession of Faith. Ironically, these amendments and a proposed "Brief Statement of Reformed Faith," designed to provide the laity with a summary of the Reformed tradition, addressed the very issues over which the Cumberland Presbyterians had withdrawn in 1810. Indeed, to many Cumberland ministers, the adoption of these amendments appeared to symbolize something of a recantation. To these observers, the Northern church had finally seen the wisdom of the Cumberland revivalist patriarchs and were now willing to modify the harshness of traditional Calvinism and heal a historic breach of fellowship.[28] But the Presbyterian Church U.S.A. was not the only party that would be required to offer theological compromises in the merger. By the opening of the twentieth century, many Northern Presbyterian ministers had drunk deeply from the well of "modernism"—a species of theological liberalism that would likely offend traditional Cumberland sensibilities. Both the Cumberland church and the Presbyterian Church U.S.A. also saw the merger as an opportunity to become truly national bodies. Given the Presbyterian Church U.S.A.'s Northern strength, and the Cumberland church's established work in the South, both parties saw the merger as a way to widen their geographic influence and end their often-parochial regionalism.

Although the merger offered an opportunity to breach the theological and regional divisions between two major Presbyterian bodies, it also posed a dilemma that would become a social litmus test for both denominations. During Reconstruction, Northern missionary endeavors in the South had produced a number of black Presbyterian congregations. At the opening of the twentieth century these local bodies were gathered into thirteen black presbyteries. Stretching from Virginia to Mississippi and from North Carolina to the Indian Territory, these segregated presbyteries—among the very few Presbyterian Church U.S.A. presbyteries in the American South—occupied the same regions as did white Cumberland presbyteries. Because the merger did not include the Cumberland Presbyterian Church, Colored, the segregation question quickly became an important issue in the merger negotiations. Would the churches considering merger leave things unchanged and acquiesce in the policy of ecclesiastical segregation, or would they use the merger negotiations as an occasion to integrate the budding national denomination? Would Presbyterians in the merged church remain segregated, or would the Cumberland presbyteries be required to unite with the black presbyteries of the Presbyterian Church U.S.A.?

By the time the merger talks were underway, the Northern Presbyterians had already taken up the question of racially segregated presbyteries; their 1903 Assembly had formed a special committee on the Territorial Limits of Presbyteries to study the matter. Historically, the church did *not* allow the boundaries of two presbyteries to overlap. Despite the official policy, however, several presbyteries were in technical violation of the rule, particularly in situations in which one of the presbyteries in question used a language other than English. With merger looming on the horizon, the question became whether the church would grant official exceptions to the rule on the basis of race.

Although the committee apparently recognized the gravity of the problem it had been charged to solve, it took a decidedly conservative stance. In its 1904 report to the Assembly the committee defended the standing Cumberland policy of ecclesiastical segregation. They concluded that it would be "wise to allow our colored ministers and churches to be organized into separate Presbyteries, if they so desire."[29] Their reasoning for this decision was self-consciously based on the existing patterns of racial discrimination in the churches: "Say what you please about the evils of social prejudice and racial antipathies, the fact remains that the white churches will not associate themselves with colored Presbyteries."[30] The Assembly supported the recommendation of the committee and amended the policy of the church so that "in exceptional cases a Presbytery may be organized within the boundaries of existing Presbyteries, in the interest of ministers and churches speaking other than the English language, or of those of a particular race; but in no case without their consent, and the same rule shall apply to Synods."[31] This decision, hailed by many Cumberland Presbyterians as a judicious solution to a thorny social problem, became an integral part of the Basis of Union, a plan that issued in the final merger of the two bodies in 1906.[32]

In hindsight it is clear that the merger, notwithstanding its genuine successes, exacted heavy costs. In order to become a truly national church, the Presbyterian Church in the United States of America had capitulated to the reigning policy of racial segregation. It would be another half century before either the Presbyterian Church in the United States of America, or its Southern counterpart, the Presbyterian Church in the United States, would find the strength to exorcise the demon of ecclesiastical racial segregation.

NOTES

1. For more information on the development of New School Presbyterianism, see George M. Marsden, *The Evangelical Mind and the New School Presbyterian Experience: A Case Study of Thought and Theology in Nineteenth-Century America* (New Haven, Conn.: Yale University Press, 1970).

2. Sydney E. Ahlstrom, *A Religious History of the American People* (New Haven, Conn.: Yale University Press, 1972), p. 433.

3. For more detailed accounts of the frontier revivals, see Ahlstrom, *Religious History*, pp. 429ff; Ben M. Barrus, Milton L. Baughn, and Thomas H. Campbell, *A People Called Cumberland Presbyterians* (Memphis, Tenn.: Frontier Press, 1972), pp. 33ff; Dickson D. Bruce, Jr., *And They All Sang Hallelujah: Plain-Folk Camp-Meeting Religion, 1800–1845* (Knoxville: University of Tennessee Press, 1974); John B. Boles, *The Great Revival, 1787–1805* (Lexington: University Press of Kentucky, 1972); and Paul K. Conkin, *Cane Ridge: America's Pentecost* (Madison: University of Wisconsin Press, 1990).

4. For a detailed treatment of the development of Presbyterianism in Kentucky, see Louis Weeks, *Kentucky Presbyterians* (Atlanta: John Knox Press, 1983).

5. For an extensive treatment of this controversy see Barrus, et al., *People Called Cumberland Presbyterians*, pp. 51ff.

6. Ibid., p. 76.

7. Ibid., pp. 81–82.

8. These demographic data are contained in Lefferts A. Loetscher, *A Brief History of the Presbyterians*, 4th ed. (Philadelphia: Westminster Press, 1978).

9. Ernest Trice Thompson, *Presbyterians in the South*, 3 vols. (Richmond, Va.: John Knox Press, 1963–1973), 1:542.

10. Ibid., 1:542–550. For more data on the United Synod, see Harold M. Parker, Jr., *The United Synod of the South: The Southern New School Presbyterian Church* (Westport, Conn.: Greenwood Press, 1988).

11. See T. Watson Street, *The Story of Southern Presbyterians* (Richmond, Va.: John Knox Press, 1961), pp. 48ff.

12. The complex theological debates about polity questions between Northern and Southern Presbyterians are treated in some detail in Thompson, *Presbyterians in the South*, 1:510ff.

13. For an incisive treatment of the division of the churches during the antebellum period, see Clarence C. Goen, *Broken Churches, Broken Nation: Denominational Schisms and the Coming of the Civil War* (Macon, Ga.: Mercer University Press, 1985).

14. Thompson, *Presbyterians in the South*, 2:30ff.

15. Ibid., 2:30.

16. Ibid., 2:32.

17. Ibid., 2:33.

18. Andrew E. Murray, *Presbyterians and the Negro—A History* (Philadelphia: Presbyterian Historical Society, 1966), pp. 32ff.

19. See ibid., p. 42, and Gayraud S. Wilmore, *Black and Presbyterian: The Heritage and the Hope* (Philadelphia: Geneva Press, 1983), passim, for an extensive treatment of African-American Presbyterians.

20. Wilmore, *Black and Presbyterian*, pp. 67–68.

21. For more information on Jones, see Murray, *Presbyterians and the Negro*, p. 55, and Albert J. Raboteau, *Slave Religion: The "Invisible Institution" in the Antebellum South* (New York: Oxford University Press, 1978).

22. Murray, *Presbyterians and the Negro*, pp. 147–148.

23. See ibid., pp. 150ff, for details.

24. See Barrus, et al., *People Called Cumberland Presbyterians*, pp. 151ff.

25. Ahlstrom, *Religious History*, p. 767.

26. George M. Marsden, *Fundamentalism and American Culture: The Shaping of Twentieth-Century Evangelicalism, 1870–1925* (New York: Oxford University Press, 1980), p. 111.

27. See Thompson, *Presbyterians in the South*, 2:457ff, for the details of the debate between Woodrow and Dabney.

28. See Barrus, et al., *People Called Cumberland Presbyterians*, pp. 323ff, for the details of the amendments and the Cumberland reaction to them.

29. *Minutes of the General Assembly of the Presbyterian Church in the United States of America* (Philadelphia: Office of the General Assembly, 1904), p. 145.

30. Ibid., p. 146.

31. Ibid., pp. 146–147.

32. For details of the merger from the perspective of the Cumberland Church, see Barrus, et al., *People Called Cumberland Presbyterians*, pp. 336ff.

5
AMERICAN PRESBYTERIANISM TO THE MID-TWENTIETH CENTURY

Many Protestants found the decades surrounding the turn of the century disorienting. Urbanization and industrialization, especially in the North, altered the character of the American population and, by extension, the composition of Protestant denominations. More important, a huge influx of immigrants, most of them Catholic or Jewish, threatened the hegemony of American Protestantism. Finally, several intellectual currents threatened to overwhelm traditional Protestant understandings of the Bible. Pushed to their logical extremes, the ideas of Charles Darwin, published in *The Origin of Species* in 1859, discredited literal readings of Scripture. The discipline of higher criticism, emanating from Germany, challenged the hitherto accepted wisdom about the provenance and authorship of sacred texts.

American Presbyterians felt the repercussions of these developments even more acutely than other Protestant denominations. By the 1920s, when Northern Presbyterians were riven by spectacular intradenominational battles, the skirmishes between liberals and conservatives of the previous century looked exceedingly tame by comparison.

THE SOCIAL GOSPEL

In the three decades between 1860 and 1890 the population of New York, Philadelphia, and Baltimore doubled; Kansas City and Detroit grew fourfold; Chicago tenfold; Los Angeles twentyfold; the populations of both Omaha and Minneapolis in 1890 were fifty times greater than what they had been in 1860. For American Protestants, then, the cities presented both opportunity and danger—opportunities for evangelism and social amelioration amid the dangers of increasing labor unrest and class tensions.

What became abundantly clear by 1900 was that America's cities were not exactly Protestant strongholds. Whereas Roman Catholics numbered only thirty thousand in 1790, the Catholic population in the United States reached twelve million in 1900. Immigrants, especially from southern and eastern Europe, clustered into ethnic ghettos. Despite the urban awakening of 1858 that had brought evangelical piety to urban precincts, by the end of the century Protestant churches were steadily losing influence in the cities. Jacob Riis, in *How the Other Half Lives*, published in 1890, characterized the urban situation as a losing battle for Protestantism:

Where God builds a church the devil builds next door a saloon, is an old saying that has lost its point in New York. Either the devil was on the ground first, or he has been doing a good deal more in the way of building. I tried once to find out how the account stood, and counted 111 Protestant churches, chapels and places of worship of every kind below Fourteenth Street, 4,065 saloons. The worst half of the tenement population lives down there, and it has to this day the worst half of the saloons. Uptown the account stands a little better, but there are easily ten saloons to every church today. I am afraid, too, that the congregations are larger by a good deal; certainly the attendance is steadier and the contributions more liberal the week round, Sunday included.[1]

Many Protestants found it easy to blame the Catholics for this dissolution, and indeed at various points in the nineteenth century they supported a number of nativist movements such as the American Protestant Association, the American Protective Association, and the Order of the Star-Spangled Banner, better known as the Know-Nothing party.

Other Protestants, however, focused on the opportunity afforded by this situation rather than the danger. Their approach became known as the Social Gospel (or Social Christianity), and it began with an assessment of the social forces that lay behind the plight of the working classes. Industrialization and unrestrained capitalism had concentrated great wealth in the hands of a few; 10 percent of the nation's families had accumulated 90 percent of the nation's wealth, and the vast labor force, drawn largely from immigrants, was not allowed to share in that prosperity. Instead, they worked twelve-hour days seven days a week, often in sweat shops, and then came home to squalid tenements afflicted with disease, drunkenness, and prostitution. The infant mortality rate in some neighborhoods approached 20 percent, and those children who survived into adolescence also faced long days of hard labor.

These conditions gave rise to burgeoning unrest and a simmering class war. Activists sought to unionize the workers who confronted industrialists in the railroad strike of 1877, the Haymarket riot of 1886 in Chicago, and the Homestead and Pullman strikes in the early 1890s. Conservative Protestants, rooted in small towns and rural areas, preferred to ignore these problems and often defended the business community. They resisted socialistic solutions and concentrated their efforts on individual regeneration. Liberal Protestants, on the other hand, sought to apply sociological and economic principles to the conditions of the city. Advocates of the Social Gospel believed that the causes, not merely the symptoms, of urban unrest had to be addressed. The biblical gospel, they maintained, redeems sinful social structures as well as sinful lives.

Although the best-known leaders and apologists of the movement came from other denominations—Washington Gladden and Josiah Strong were Congregationalists, Walter Rauschenbusch was Baptist, and Richard T. Ely was an Episcopal layman—Presbyterians could point to their own involvement as well. Late in the nineteenth century Presbyterians had organized various evangelistic outreaches and settlement houses for new immigrants. After the turn of the century Northern Presbyterians began to imbibe some of the ideas of the Social Gospel. In 1903 they created a Workingmen's Department and supported the Labor Temple in New York City. The General Assembly of 1910 outlined a series of moral goals for industry, aimed at protecting the integrity of the individual worker.

WORLD WAR I AND AMERICAN PRESBYTERIANS

Although the destinies of all America, even the world, were tied up with the conflict brewing in Europe, American Presbyterians had perhaps a special stake in that one of their own, President Woodrow Wilson,* guided the nation during those perilous years. In addition, another prominent Presbyterian layman, Robert E. Speer,* secretary of the Board of Foreign Missions of the Presbyterian Church U.S.A., also chaired the General War-Time Commission, operated by the Federal Council of Churches. Wilson's, of course, was the greater task, and he forcefully articulated America's mandate in World War I: "Make the world safe for democracy." That is not to say, of course, that all Presbyterians agreed with Wilson on the necessity of the war effort (or on other policies); indeed, a fair number, including William Jennings Bryan,* Wilson's secretary of state until 1915, embraced pacifism and opposed America's entry into the "Great War."

Many theologically conservative Presbyterians, however, used the occasion of war to unite the strands of American patriotism and theological conservatism. Firebrand Presbyterian evangelist William A. (Billy) Sunday,* for instance, conducted "Hang the Kaiser" rallies and pointed to Germany as the source of what he regarded as pernicious liberal theological notions. "If you turn hell upside down," Sunday blustered, "you will find 'Made in Germany' stamped on the bottom."[2] Other, less hysterical voices joined Sunday in equating Germany with infidelity. The editor of the *Presbyterian* also decried theological liberalism as a product of Germany and declared that it needed to be repudiated as forcefully as German imperialism.[3]

FUNDAMENTALIST–MODERNIST CONTROVERSY

Just as so many of the disputes afflicting American Presbyterians had revolved around the Westminster standards, so too the fundamentalist–modernist controversy, which profoundly divided Presbyterians in the twentieth century, involved a disagreement over Westminster. The subscription controversy in the eighteenth century, eventually settled by the Adopting Act of 1729, pitted strict confessionalists from the Middle Colonies against the Presbyterians from New England and from the English Puritan traditions who were less concerned about strict subscription to Westminster than they were about heartfelt piety. In the wake of the revivals early in the nineteenth century, Old School Presbyterians, whose strength lay in Pennsylvania, the South, and at Princeton Theological Seminary, deplored what they regarded as laxity in the doctrinal matters covered by the Westminster standards, while the New School, quite popular in New York and in the West, worried more about refining revival techniques and adapting harsh Calvinist doctrines to an age enamored of self-determinism.

By the closing decades of the nineteenth century, the Princetonians, relying on the Scottish common sense philosophy brought to America by John Witherspoon,* had developed a strong affinity for propositional truth, especially those propositions set forth in the Westminster standards, which Princeton viewed as a generally trustworthy distillation of the truths of the Bible, impervious to change, and readily apparent to any openminded seeker. This is not to suggest that the Princetonians were unfeeling confessionalists; indeed, they promoted lively piety among their students. In a preface to a collection of his father's sermons, A. A. Hodge* recalled Sunday afternoon meetings at Princeton Seminary where "dry and cold attributes of scientific theology, moving in the sphere of the intellect, gave place to the warmth of personal religious experience, and to the spiritual light of divinely illuminated intuition." At the same time, however, Princeton theologians, and Charles Hodge* in particular, were eager to modify Friedrich Schleiermacher's claim that true religion was grounded in an awareness of absolute dependence on God. For them, reason and spiritual experience worked together in the life of faith, and neither should be permitted to prevail over the other. Truth was not, they insisted, historically relative, as Charles Briggs* and others held, and the Bible not only *contained* the Word of God, it *was* the Word of God. Princeton's insistence on this point issued in various attempts to have the General Assembly reaffirm biblical inerrancy. In the midst of the Briggs heresy trials of the early 1890s, the General Assembly, meeting in Portland, Oregon, in 1892, declared that the original manuscripts of the Bible were "without error." The Assembly reaffirmed this so-called Portland Deliverance the following year.

Moderate Presbyterians early in the 1890s attempted to revise the Confession of Faith. At the 1889 General Assembly fifteen presbyteries had presented memorials asking for a revision of the Westminster Confession of Faith, but the proposed revisions presented the following year failed to garner the necessary two-thirds approval. Conservatives were especially chary about conceding ground on the Confession while they were pursuing the conviction of Briggs, who at his third trial was finally convicted of heresy in 1893. Conservatives also initiated action against Henry Preserved Smith* and Arthur Cushman McGiffert* for their progressive views, their departure from orthodox Calvinism, and for what conservatives regarded as their denial of biblical inerrancy. By 1900 all three had been drummed out of the denomination, thereby vindicating the exercise of formal ecclesiastical action against "heresy."

Calls for creedal revision continued, however. The General Assembly of 1900 appointed a "Committee of Fifteen" to make recommendations the following year. Once again, moderates and liberals tended to support some kind of revision, while conservatives refused. Benjamin B. Warfield* of Princeton Seminary, for instance, declined an invitation to serve on the committee. "It is an inexpressible grief to me," he wrote, to see the church "spending its energies in a vain attempt to lower its testimony to suit the ever changing sentiment of the world about it."[4] Northern Presbyterians finally adopted eleven relatively tame overtures at the General Assembly in 1903, including statements on missions and on the Holy Spirit, an affirmation of God's love for all humanity, and the assurance of salvation for those dying in infancy.

This action, however, did not placate the growing demands for a more contemporary statement of faith. The General Assembly of 1910, responding to complaints about doctrinal laxity on the part of three Union Seminary graduates, adopted a set of five "essential and necessary" doctrines at its closing session, after many of the delegates had left. These doctrines included belief in the inerrancy of the Bible; the virgin birth of Christ; his substitutionary atonement; Christ's bodily resurrection; and the authenticity of miracles. The General Assembly reaffirmed these "essentials" in 1916 and 1923, and they became the "famous five points" of contention among Presbyterians in the 1920s.

More important, however, these five essential doctrines paralleled the "five points of fundamentalism," growing out of the 1895 Niagara Bible Conference, with the exception that fundamentalists had insisted on premillennialism rather than the authenticity of miracles. As conservative Presbyterians felt more and more beleaguered, they began to look for allies outside the Presbyterian Church U.S.A. They found kindred spirits in the emerging, interdenominational coalition of conservative Protestants who became known as fundamentalists, named after the series of twelve booklets called, collectively, *The Fundamentals: A Testimony to the Truth*, published from 1910 to 1915 and financed by Union Oil tycoons Lyman and Milton Stewart of California.

During the 1910s, however, conservatives within the Presbyterian Church U.S.A. carried out their denominational battles largely unaided by the broader fundamentalist coalition. When David S. Kennedy assumed the editorship of *The Presbyterian* in 1911, he titled his first editorial "The Present Conflict" and wrote that the battle shaping up between conservatives and liberals (or fundamentalists and modernists) was "the renewal of the old primitive conflict between cultured heathenism and historic Christianity."[5] Harry Emerson Fosdick,* a graduate of Union Theological Seminary, laid down the gauntlet to battle with a widely circulated sermon titled "Shall the Fundamentalists Win?" preached on 21 May 1922 from the pulpit of First Presbyterian Church in New York City, where Fosdick, a Baptist, served as associate pastor. In what Fosdick's

biographer says was "the most far-reaching sermon of his career," Fosdick
argued that liberalism was certainly a legitimate form of Christianity and that
fundamentalists could not "drive out from the Christian churches all the consecrated souls who do not agree with their theory of inspiration." Moreover,
Fosdick continued, "just now the Fundamentalists are giving us one of the worst
exhibitions of bitter intolerance that the churches of this country have ever seen."[6]

Conservative Presbyterians responded to Fosdick's taunt and to his expressed
doubts about the virgin birth, the inerrancy of the Scriptures and the second
coming of Christ. *The Presbyterian* rejoined by printing a sermon titled "Shall
Unbelief Win?" Even William Jennings Bryan, the "Great Commoner," former
secretary of state and three-time presidential candidate, entered the fray with his
1922 treatise *In His Image: An Answer to Darwinism*, which attacked Fosdick's
theistic evolution. Darwinism, Bryan argued, represented the first major menace
to Christianity since the birth of Christ. The Presbytery of Philadelphia, meeting
in the home of John Wanamaker,* adopted an overture to the General Assembly,
urging it "to direct the Presbytery of New York to take such action as will
require the preaching and teaching in the First Presbyterian Church of New York
City to conform to the system of doctrine taught in the Confession of Faith."[7]
By a vote of 439 to 359, the Assembly of 1923 agreed and, at the same time,
reaffirmed the five-point doctrinal statement of 1910.

The fundamentalists' most biting attack on liberalism within the Presbyterian
Church U.S.A. came from the pen of J. Gresham Machen,* a gifted professor
of New Testament at Princeton Theological Seminary. In *Christianity and Liberalism*, published in 1923, Machen argued that liberalism, despite its traditional
phraseology, was not some harmless variant of Christianity; it was, in fact, not
Christianity at all but a new and different religion. The two ideologies, then,
were fundamentally incompatible, according to Machen, and could not dwell
together within the same church. He called on liberals to do the only honorable
thing—withdraw from the church so that the "true Christians," the conservatives, could perpetuate the historical doctrines of Christianity without impedi-
ment. According to Machen, moreover, reconciliation of these two radically
different religions would be impossible, and if liberals refused to withdraw, then
the conservatives would be obliged to do so, whatever the sacrifice.

In January 1924 a group of 150 Presbyterian clergy signed *An Affirmation*
popularly known as the "Auburn Affirmation," which was republished in May
of the same year with 1,274 signatures. While the Affirmation ratified the doctrines embraced by the five-point declaration of the 1910 General Assembly, it
also allowed that some within the denomination might have other, equally valid
formulae for explaining these truths. The signers of the Affirmation, then, urged
tolerance within the denomination for those who might affirm alternative explanations of Christian doctrines. The signatories were "united in believing that
these are not the only theories allowed by the Scriptures and our standards as
explanations of these facts and doctrines of our religion, and that all who hold

to these facts and doctrines, whatever theories they may employ to explain them, are worthy of all confidence and fellowship."[8]

Presbyterian fundamentalists were slow to recognize the threat embodied in the Auburn Affirmation, and they pursued their agenda through other channels. In the 1925 General Assembly the conservatives prevailed in what was, in effect, a reprimand of the New York Presbytery for ordaining ministerial candidates who held equivocal views on the virgin birth of Christ. In response, Henry Sloane Coffin,* speaking for the presbytery, threatened to leave the denomination if the judgment was not overturned. The Assembly then, at the behest of its moderator, Charles R. Erdman,* resolved to appoint a "Commission of Fifteen" to study "the causes making for unrest" within the denomination and report back to the next Assembly.[9]

The commission's report to the 1926 General Assembly repudiated Machen's contention that conservativism and liberalism were mutually exclusive religions. The commission came out solidly in favor of toleration within the denomination, asserting that "the Presbyterian system admits diversity of view where the core of truth is identical."[10] The commission also severely circumscribed the powers of the General Assembly to define doctrine, thereby effectively nullifying the five-point declaration of "essential" doctrines and bringing the matter of doctrinal conformity in line with the Auburn Affirmation. When the report of the commission was adopted by the Assembly, conservative Presbyterians were suddenly placed on the defensive.

FUNDAMENTALISM, MODERNISM, AND DIVISION

Princeton Theological Seminary, once the bastion of Presbyterian conservatism, became the next battleground between fundamentalism and modernism. By the 1920s a rift between the two camps had developed within the faculty. Early in May 1926 the board of directors had elected Machen to the chair of apologetics and ethics, an action confirmed by the trustees. The votes were far from unanimous, however, and a number of directors and trustees asked the General Assembly to investigate the divisions at the seminary. The Assembly deferred confirmation of Machen's election to the chair pending the findings of still another committee, this one appointed to study the seminary. In its report to the General Assembly of 1927 the committee deftly sidestepped the theological issues at the root of the dispute and recommended instead the appointment of an expanded committee to supervise the reorganization of Princeton Theological Seminary. After countless debates, studies, and majority and minority reports, the Assembly of 1929 finally altered the seminary's organization to place it under the supervision of a single board.

Machen, still denied the chair of apologetics, interpreted this reorganization as an unalloyed victory for the forces of modernism. He and his fundamentalist colleagues promptly withdrew from Princeton and on 25 September 1929 opened

Westminster Seminary in Philadelphia with fifty-two students and a faculty of eight. Another succession soon followed. Reacting once again to the perceived drift toward liberalism within the Presbyterian Church U.S.A., Machen and other conservatives formed the Independent Board for Presbyterian Foreign Missions in October 1933. Under the guidance of Charles Woodbridge, its first secretary, the board declared that it would be "organized by Bible-believing Christians to promote truly Biblical and truly Presbyterian mission work."[11]

By the mid-1930s it was becoming increasingly clear that fundamentalists were losing ground not only among Northern Presbyterians but within other mainline denominations and in the broader culture as well. The infamous 1925 "monkey trial" of John T. Scopes in Dayton, Tennessee, seriously discredited the fundamentalist cause. Although Scopes was convicted and fined $100 for violating the Butler Act, which forbade the teaching of evolution in public schools (the conviction was later overturned on a technicality), fundamentalists lost the larger battle for public sentiment. Clarence Darrow's wry and spirited cross-examination of William Jennings Bryan, who served as counsel for the prosecution, together with H. L. Mencken's stinging dispatches from Dayton lampooning fundamentalists as backwoods country bumpkins, succeeded in discrediting fundamentalism and attaching a stigma that persists to this day.

Within the Presbyterian Church U.S.A. conservative influence steadily waned, and soon Machen himself faced disciplinary charges for his separatist tendencies. The General Assembly of 1934 had directed that Machen's Independent Board cease functioning within the denomination and that all Presbyterians sever their ties to the board. On 29 March 1935 the Presbytery of New Brunswick suspended Machen's ordination "until such time as he shall give satisfactory evidence of repentance."[12] The General Assembly also approved the censure of other Presbyterians who had affiliated with the Independent Board.

On 11 June 1936 Machen and his fellow conservatives formed their own ecclesiastical body, the Presbyterian Church of America, which changed its name three years later to the Orthodox Presbyterian Church. Machen was elected the first moderator of the denomination, whereupon he declared that the new organization was a "true Presbyterian church at last."[13] Ironically, the separatist proclivities of the fundamentalists precipitated still another division within their own ranks. Machen died of pneumonia on 1 January 1937, leaving his fragile coalition of conservatives without a leader who could hold it together. Later that year, exactly one hundred years after the New School–Old School schism of 1837, a number of ministers, led by Carl T. McIntire,* left the Presbyterian Church in America to form the even more radically separatist denomination that would be known as the Bible Presbyterian Church.[14]

FUNDAMENTALISM IN THE SOUTH

Southern Presbyterianism, officially known as the Presbyterian Church in the United States, was affected far less by the fundamentalist–modernist controversy that raged in the North. This was due in part to the fact that liberal ideas were far less prevalent in the South and therefore did not represent a threat to the overwhelming conservatism of the Presbyterian Church U.S. clergy. Moreover, the distinctly southern, Old School notion of the "spirituality of the church" tended to keep southern Presbyterians from engaging in the broader cultural aspects of the fundamentalist controversy. There were some rumblings of unrest, however. William Caldwell of the First Presbyterian Church in Fort Worth, Texas, and F. E. Maddox of First Church in Texarkana, Arkansas, both ran afoul of their presbyteries for holding "modernist" doctrines and liberal views of the Bible. Caldwell survived the challenge, but Maddox, who openly disputed the doctrine of the plenary inspiration of the Scriptures and insisted that he was "preaching Calvinism as John Calvin would preach it if he were living in this day," was suspended by the Ouachita Presbytery and left the denomination to form a Congregational church in Texarkana.[15] Henry M. Edmonds of South Highlands Church in Birmingham left the North Alabama Presbytery when his orthodoxy was challenged and, together with about two hundred members of his former congregation, organized the Independent Presbyterian Church of Birmingham. Another minister, D. Witherspoon Dodge of the Piedmont Presbytery, was deposed in 1917 for his departures from orthodox Calvinism.

Southern Presbyterians invested more energy in the struggle against Darwinism, thereby continuing the nineteenth-century battles waged by Robert L. Dabney* against James Woodrow* and others sympathetic to evolutionary theory. Many Presbyterians vigorously sought the passage of laws banning the teaching of evolution in the public schools. One of the most important battlegrounds was North Carolina, where Southern Presbyterians, lay and clerical, played important roles in an unsuccessful effort to persuade the legislature to pass such a restriction on tax-supported institutions in that state. Having failed on that front, the opponents of Darwinism turned their guns on those within the denomination who supported theistic evolution.

In 1923 the *Presbyterian Standard* warned that "there is an epidemic of heresy, not only in churches where it has shown itself at intervals in the past, but also incipient in our own ranks—and with the least encouragement it will break into open rebellion."[16] Indeed, a growing chorus of pastors and scholars within the Presbyterian Church U.S. began increasingly to challenge conservative assumptions about inspiration and inerrancy. Those who sought some loosening of conservative strictures in the South also began to advocate acceptance of some of the findings of the higher critics, reconsideration of the doctrine of innate depravity, and even union with the Presbyterian Church U.S.A. Conservatives responded with desultory attempts to persuade ecclesiastical tribunals to examine the views of those suspected of departing from the faith. On the whole, however, the presbyteries refused to do so, and Southern Presbyterians thereby escaped the rancor that such purges had caused in the North.

RE-THINKING PRESBYTERIAN MISSIONS

The fundamentalist–modernist controversy, however, did have far-reaching implications, in both North and South. In 1930 the Laymen's Foreign Missions

Inquiry, with the financial backing of John D. Rockefeller, Jr., and the support of seven denominations, including the Presbyterian Church U.S.A., undertook a study of Protestant foreign missions. The findings were then entrusted to a commission, chaired by William Ernest Hocking, Alford Professor of Philosophy at Harvard University, which issued a seven-volume assessment of Protestant missions, together with detailed recommendations.

Coming on the heels of the fundamentalist–modernist controversies of the previous decade, the commission's report, especially its one-volume summary titled *Re-Thinking Missions*, attracted enormous attention in Protestant circles. "There is a growing conviction that the mission enterprise is at a fork in the road," the report began, "and that momentous decisions are called for."[17] Reflecting the generally liberal theological sentiments of Hocking and the rest of the commission and building upon earlier calls for ecumenicity, *Re-Thinking Missions* urged a recasting of missions in light of "the many changes in the world during the past century."[18]

First, the commission called attention to an "altered theological outlook" within the Western churches. Western Christianity had shifted "its stress from the negative to the affirmative side of its message"; it was now "less a religion of fear and more a religion of beneficence."[19] These changes were largely theological; modern Christians, the report claimed, were not apt to mouth traditional claims about the everlasting torments of hell, God's punitive justice, or similar "otherworldly"—all of which had given "the original motive of Protestant missions much of its urgency."[20] In a backhanded stab at the fundamentalists, the report declared triumphantly that western Christianity had "passed through and beyond the stage of bitter conflict with the scientific consciousness of the race over details of the mode of creation, the age of the earth, the descent of man, miracle and law, to the stage of maturity in which a free religion and a free science become inseparable and complementary elements in a complete world-view." Despite these progressive trends, however, Christianity still suffered "from the poverty, the rigidity, the inertness of the conceptions which Christians have of its significance."[21] The report urged greater respect for the validity and integrity of other religions, cast serious doubts on the quality of missionaries in the field, and urged that "a much more critical selection of candidates should be made, even at the risk of curtailing the number of missionaries sent out."[22]

Predictably, *Re-Thinking Missions* caused a stir among foreign missionaries and the congregations and boards that supported them. Perhaps one of the most controversial responses to the Hocking Report came from Pearl S. Buck,* a novelist who was the daughter of missionaries and wife of a Presbyterian missionary to China. Buck had returned to the United States on furlough about the time the Hocking Report was released. Asked by the *Christian Century* to review the volume, Beck wrote a lengthy and quite laudatory essay hailing it as "a masterpiece of constructive religious thought" imbued with a "spirit which to me is nothing less than inspired."[23]

Buck's opinions gained a wide hearing, not least because of her emerging fame as a novelist; *The Good Earth* was published in 1931 and won the Pulitzer Prize in 1932. She elaborated her views on missions in an address before Presbyterian women and missions officials at the Astor Hotel in New York City. Her speech was reprinted as "Is There a Case for Foreign Missions?" in the January 1933 issue of *Harper's*. Buck's response to her own rhetorical question was a qualified "yes." After cataloging the sins and the insensitivities of missionaries she had known, Buck chided American Protestants for sending such "little men and women" to the mission field, while keeping the best for service at home, and for judging the effectiveness of missionaries on the basis of numbers of converts and church members.[24]

Buck's strident criticisms of mission policy both echoed and built upon the findings of the Hocking Commission. Not all Presbyterians found *Re-Thinking Missions* so laudable, however. Robert Speer, author of an essay in the *Fundamentals* series, secretary of the Presbyterian Board of Foreign Missions, and the most prominent Presbyterian missionary spokesperson of the day, issued a generally balanced assessment, although he remained suspicious of the commission's more liberal sentiments.[25] J. Gresham Machen, having recently bolted from Princeton to form Westminster Seminary, considered the commission's report beneath contempt; it represented, he claimed, an attack "against the very heart of the Christian religion."[26]

Re-Thinking Missions and immediate Presbyterian reactions to it rekindled an old controversy in Presbyterian circles. In 1921 W. H. Griffith Thomas, an Episcopalian, had addressed the Presbyterian Social Union of Philadelphia and charged that a number of missionaries to China, including some Presbyterians, were sympathetic to higher criticism and modernism. This development he traced to an influx of graduates from liberal seminaries and to a desire on the part of those on the mission field to show the compatibility of Christianity with other religions. Even though he refused to identify individual missionaries guilty of holding modernist ideas, Thomas's charges created a brief stir among Presbyterians until Speer and others were able to offer reassurances about the reliability and orthodoxy of Presbyterian missionaries.

Re-Thinking Missions and Buck's assessment of it, however, revived Presbyterian suspicions, and in 1934 the Presbyterian Church U.S.A. formally disavowed "those parts of the volume *Re-Thinking Missions* which are not in harmony with New Testament teachings and not in agreement with the doctrinal position of the Presbyterian Church."[27] Although the Southern church, the Presbyterian Church U.S., had not been a constituent member of the Hocking study, their Standing Committee on Foreign Missions did not hesitate to offer the following venomous response to presbyters gathered at their 1935 Assembly: "With utmost emphasis we repudiate that monumental folly miscalled 'Rethinking Missions.' Its true title should rather be: 'Rejecting Missions and Crucifying Our Lord Afresh.' It offers a bread and milk poultice for the bite of the deadly cobra."[28]

Despite this storm of controversy in the 1930s, the story of Presbyterian missions over the next four decades can be interpreted as a gradual process in which American Presbyterians adopted the proposals set forth in *Re-Thinking Missions*. By the later decades of the twentieth century Presbyterian missions policy, both North and South, would become openly critical of American imperialism and concern itself less with soul-winning than with ecumenical cooperation, social justice, and the establishment of indigenous churches.

Beset by theological controversy, riven by ecclesiastical schism, and faced with rapidly changing social realities, the first half of the twentieth century proved to be a time of trial for American Presbyterians. Presbyterians in the American North found themselves divided over theological issues. While one party chose to accommodate itself and its theology to the new intellectual currents and the novel social conditions of the twentieth century, the other party allied itself ever more closely to the seventeenth-century verities of Westminster and to a biblical hermeneutic that insisted on the inerrancy of Scripture. By the 1930s the two parties found their differences irreconcilable and went their separate ways. Presbyterians in the American South also faced great challenges. Though they managed to avoid the debilitating effects of the famed "fundamentalist–modernist controversy," by mid-century Southern Presbyterians found themselves awash in a sea of cultural change. Economic prospects improved as business and industry turned their attentions to the South. As a new South began to prosper, the Civil Rights movement was born, the turbulent sixties began, and the Old South became a thing of the past.

NOTES

1. Quoted in Edwin Scott Gaustad, *A Religious History of America* (New York: Harper & Row, 1966), p. 245.

2. Quoted in George M. Marsden, *Fundamentalism and American Culture: The Shaping of Twentieth-Century Evangelicalism, 1870–1925* (New York: Oxford University Press, 1980), p. 142.

3. Lefferts A. Loetscher, *The Broadening Church: A Study of the Theological Issues in the Presbyterian Church Since 1869* (Philadelphia: University of Pennsylvania Press, 1954), p. 103.

4. Quoted in ibid., p. 83.

5. Quoted in ibid., p. 102.

6. Robert Moats Miller, *Harry Emerson Fosdick: Preacher, Pastor, Prophet* (New York: Oxford University Press, 1985), pp. 115–116. Fosdick's sermon was widely circulated under the title "The New Knowledge and the Christian Faith."

7. Quoted in ibid., p. 119.

8. Quoted in Loetscher, *Broadening Church*, p. 118.

9. Quoted in ibid., p. 128.

10. Quoted in ibid., p. 131.

11. Quoted in ibid., p. 150.

12. Quoted in ibid., p. 152.

13. Quoted in Marsden, *Fundamentalism and American Culture*, p. 192.

14. For the details of this schism, see idem, "Perspective on the Division of 1837," in *Pressing Toward the Mark: Essays Commemorating Fifty Years of the Orthodox Presbyterian Church*, ed. Charles G. Dennison and Richard C. Gamble (Philadelphia: Orthodox Presbyterian Church, 1986), chap. 18.

15. Quoted in Ernest Trice Thompson, *Presbyterians in the South*, 3 vols. (Richmond: John Knox Press, 1963–1973), 3:306.

16. Quoted in ibid., 3:325.

17. Laymen's Foreign Missions Inquiry, The Commission of Appraisal, William Ernest Hocking, Chairman, *Re-Thinking Missions: A Laymen's Inquiry After One Hundred Years* (New York: Harper & Brothers, 1932), p. ix. For a secondary treatment of the Hocking Report and the controversy it generated within American Presbyterianism, see William R. Hutchison, *Errand to the World: American Protestant Thought and Foreign Missions* (Chicago: University of Chicago Press, 1987), pp. 158–175; Gerald H. Anderson, "American Protestants in Pursuit of Mission: 1886–1986," *International Bulletin of Missionary Research* 12, no. 3 (July 1988): 106–108.

18. Hocking, *Re-Thinking Missions*, p. 18.

19. Ibid., pp. 18, 19.

20. Ibid., p. 19.

21. Ibid., pp. 19, 45.

22. Ibid., pp. 292, 327.

23. Pearl S. Buck, "The Laymen's Mission Report," *Christian Century* 49 (November 23, 1932), p. 1434.

24. Idem, "Is There a Case for Foreign Missions?" *Harper's Monthly Magazine* 166 (January 1933), p. 147.

25. Robert E. Speer, *"Re-Thinking Missions" Examined* (New York: Fleming H. Revell, 1933).

26. Hutchison, *Errand to the World*, p. 172. Buck herself faced stiff criticism in Presbyterian circles for her liberal views, and her standing eroded further when she left the mission field and divorced her husband several years later. Hutchison, *Errand to the World*, p. 169. Buck herself was not technically a Presbyterian missionary; even though she often referred to herself as a missionary, at other times she would insist that it was her *husband* who was the missionary.

27. *Minutes of General Assembly of The Presbyterian Church in the U.S.A.* (Philadelphia: Office of the General Assembly, 1934), p. 242.

28. *Minutes of the Presbyterian Church in the United States* (Richmond, Va.: Presbyterian Commission of Publications, 1935), p. 39.

6
AMERICAN PRESBYTERIANISM IN AN ECUMENICAL AGE

By the middle of the twentieth century the Presbyterian churches in America were the nation's fourth largest Protestant family, with a total membership of over four million. The decade of the 1960s, however, would bring a series of cultural challenges that would leave the nation and its churches forever changed. At home and abroad American Presbyterians discovered, to their discomfort, the extent to which their version of the good news had been allied with the American mythos. America's children seemed disaffected; they viewed with increasing skepticism a gospel that appeared to baptize freewheeling capitalism, racial and gender inequities, and traditional middle-class American values.

By 1965 the effects of this ennui were becoming apparent: Protestant denominational growth suddenly halted, and membership dropped sharply. In the United Presbyterian Church U.S.A., for instance, church membership peaked in 1965 at three-and-one-third million members; ten years later the denomination had lost more than half a million members, a decline of roughly 18 percent.[1] American Presbyterians found themselves in a new cultural and religious environment in the second half of the twentieth century. This chapter deals with how they responded to these changes and with the central problems facing the tradition as it looks beyond the 1990s into the twenty-first century.[2]

POSTWAR PRESBYTERIANISM

Buoyed by the Allied military victories in Europe and Japan, fully prepared to continue in their position as a democratic leader among the nations of the world, and confident of their ability to oversee the destiny of the nation, post–World War II Americans turned their attention to the pursuit of domestic tranquility. Millions of veterans returned to their prewar occupations, the nation's industrial systems retooled in order to accommodate growing and lucrative consumer markets, and the now famous "baby boom" guaranteed the future of middle-class America.

American churches shared in the prosperity; membership soared to all-time highs, local congregations erected new facilities, and church-related educational institutions prospered. These good times notwithstanding, however, American Presbyterians soon faced a remarkable set of cultural changes and difficult challenges to the way they viewed the nation and the world. As church historian Sydney Ahlstrom noted, the arrival of the "turbulent sixties" marked the end of a unified, four-hundred-year period in the Anglo-American experience; the terms "post-Puritan" and "post-Protestant" had become apt—and to many Americans, unsettling—historical descriptions.[3]

Although the war may not have been directly responsible for the shifting patterns within American culture, it did prepare the nation's citizens for life in the new cultural ethos. The war had bolstered some elements of the traditional American mythos—patriotism and a popular vision of American destiny—but it also led to the formation of a new understanding of the world. Millions of Americans had become familiar with different cultures around the globe. Military personnel had experienced these new worlds first-hand, and noncombatants, living out the war years vicariously through the media, also formed new views of what came to be called the "global village." Thus prepared, Americans faced a series of important developments in post–World War II international politics— the spread of Communism, the escalating war in Vietnam, and the civil rights movement—all of which began to receive attention in the General Assemblies of both the Presbyterian Church U.S.A. and the Presbyterian Church U.S.[4]

The rise of Communism and its rapid spread throughout the world was perhaps the most threatening challenge to face the American churches in the postwar period. During the war, Americans had willingly sacrificed the life blood of the nation in the Allied attempt to vanquish Nazism, fascism, and Japanese imperialism. Throughout the war the Soviet Union had been a staunch defender of the Allied cause, but after 1945—with the Allies occupying and redrawing the boundaries of Europe and with Nagasaki and Hiroshima in ruins—diplomatic relations between East and West chilled considerably. Churchill's "iron curtain" speech in March 1946, the popular use of the expression "cold war," and the media attention given to the House Committee to Investigate Un-American Activities, combined to create an atmosphere of suspicion and intrigue. Millions of patriotic Americans, and among them many Presbyterian leaders, were unabashed in their denunciations of Communism.

As early as 1948, the Missions Board of the Presbyterian Church U.S. expressed the fear that "Communism threatens with atheism and lawlessness."[5] In the Presbyterian Church U.S.A., missionary comments in 1952 were even more pointed: "We are deeply alarmed by the terrible and devastating forces of Communism and Materialism which seek to divide and conquer the world and to destroy the cherished values and institutions which Christianity has brought about."[6] From the missionaries' perspective, international Communism appeared to be preparing to "wipe Christianity from the world."[7] The missionaries' response to the crisis was singular; the churches must busy themselves "saving the world for Christ."[8] Throughout the fifties, however, that salvation was not forthcoming. Korea was rent by a civil war that pitted Communism against the forces of democracy, Soviet forces occupied large parts of Europe, thereby creating the "eastern bloc." Communist gains in China were consolidated under Mao Zedong, and Cuba fell to the Communists under the revolutionary leadership of Fidel Castro.

By 1961 tensions between East and West were dangerously high. The Berlin Wall—a visible brick-and-mortar icon of the "iron curtain"—was erected, and counter-revolutionaries, under the direction of the Central Intelligence Agency, attempted to overthrow the Castro regime at the Bay of Pigs. The Cuban missile crisis ensued the following year, and although American President John F. Kennedy and Soviet Premier Nikita Krushchev barely avoided a nuclear confrontation, the Communist threat was now alarmingly close—a mere ninety miles from United States shores. With Civil Defense organizations encouraging the erection of homemade bomb shelters, and with schoolchildren being drilled in procedures to follow in the event of a nuclear attack, the church quite naturally continued its litany of condemnation of Communism. Borrowing from the rhetoric of revolution that had become popular in international affairs, Presbyterian leaders sought to instigate their own "World Revolution—Christian style."[9] They proposed to replace Communism's "mechanistic, deterministic view of man" with the gospel, which viewed "the individual as a child of God, a person of dignity who should be free."[10] These spiritual countermeasures were designed to thwart the advance of Communism abroad. Increasingly, however, the threat of international Communism was overshadowed by a series of domestic crises closer to home.

THE WAR IN VIETNAM AND THE BATTLE FOR CIVIL RIGHTS

In a 1959 speech at Gettysburg College, President Dwight D. Eisenhower publicly affirmed his administration's commitment to help maintain South Vietnam as an independent, sovereign nation. At that time the United States had posted about 760 military troops—all of whom were to function as noncombatant military advisers—to South Vietnam. The Kennedy administration continued to provide military support for South Vietnam; by November 1963, the United States had sent over 16,000 military personnel to South Vietnam. In August 1964 Congress passed the Gulf of Tonkin Resolution, which allowed U.S. forces in Vietnam to take more aggressive action.

During the Johnson administration the number of American combat troops posted in Southeast Asia increased dramatically. By 1968, the final full year of Lyndon Johnson's presidency, troop levels peaked at over a half-million, and battle-related deaths totaled over thirty thousand.[11] Although the number of troops would steadily decline until the United States' formal withdrawal from South Vietnam in 1973, the final years of the "turbulent sixties" found the nation perplexed and angry. Despite the enormous commitment of American material and lives, and notwithstanding the attempts of three presidents to aid South Vietnam while keeping American honor intact, the war sapped the resolve of the nation.

Although a controversial war halfway around the globe became the occasion for an enormous public outcry against U.S. military policies, in these same years another crisis, whose origins were purely domestic, rent the nation. In 1954 the United States Supreme Court declared social segregation based upon race to be unconstitutional. The following year the Court mandated the desegregation of the nation's public schools, and Rosa Parks, a black seamstress from Montgomery, Alabama, refused to yield her seat on a public bus to a white man. The highly successful Montgomery bus boycott ensued, gaining national attention under the direction of Martin Luther King, Jr., and Ralph David Abernathy. In the following years the federal government formed the Civil Rights Commission, activists worked to register black voters, King delivered his famous "I Have a Dream" address, and cities across the nation erupted in violent convulsions. Indeed, by the fateful year 1968, when Dr. King and presidential candidate Robert Kennedy were assassinated, there seemed little reason to question the claim of one Presbyterian who had opined, just four years before, that America was experiencing "the most radical revolution that has taken place since the dawn of civilization."[12]

PRESBYTERIAN RESPONSES TO CULTURAL UNREST

During the 1950s and early 1960s, Presbyterian responses to the changes in the world were often negative and defensive, but by the middle of the turbulent sixties Presbyterians began to reassess their attitudes and underwent a dramatic change of consciousness: They became increasingly sensitive to the problems connected with "western" and "American imperialism," they found a new openness to the truth claims of other religions, they pursued denominational realignments designed to strengthen the Presbyterian witness in the United States, and they stressed the social dimensions of the Christian ministry with increasing vigor.

Although the threats posed by the spread of international Communism struck legitimate fears into the hearts of American citizens, Presbyterian leaders began to reflect theologically on the larger meaning of the Cold War, the perils of nuclear arms, and the realities of international political and economic diversity. The theological and intellectual seedbed for new ways of thinking about the cultural aspects of these international problems came from the missionary arms of the churches, the very groups that had initially sounded the alarm about the spread of Communism. Although Presbyterian foreign missionaries were traditionally positioned on the right of the theological spectrum, they began to translate their intimate knowledge of what it meant to appreciate unfamiliar cultures into sensitive policies that could help address the suspicions and fears that were rife in the churches.

Throughout their history, and especially during World War II, Presbyterian missionaries had patiently borne the stigma of "American imperialism." Around the globe, and with particular vehemence in the Far East, nationals on the field often interpreted missionary outreach as an attempt to convert people to Christianity *and* to American culture and social mores. This problem was first recognized in 1930 with the formation of the "Laymen's Foreign Missions Inquiry" and was fully addressed in its formal report, *Re-Thinking Missions: A Laymen's Inquiry After One Hundred Years*, published in 1932.[13] Although missionary reactions to the report were initially quite negative, Presbyterians soon implemented many of its recommendations. As early as 1947 the Presbyterian Church U.S.A. noted that it was time to "restudy the pattern of organization and the activities of the missions in their relationship to the indigenous churches" and "to transfer responsibility to the national churches."[14] These indigenous churches would become self-supporting, and each would "be able to evangelize its own people and send the Gospel to the people in regions beyond."[15] In this way, Presbyterian missionaries hoped to overcome the criticism articulated by many nationals, especially in Communist and socialist lands, that American missionaries were merely unarmed—but nonetheless dangerous—agents of American imperialism.

In the preamble to its 1955 report to the General Assembly, the Presbyterian Church U.S.A. missions board noted that one essential task of the church was to foster the healing of the nations. Recognizing that the political and cultural situations in the world were complex and often unstable, the preamble urged the church to acknowledge its former imperialism and to affirm, in a spirit of hope and expectancy, the emergence of new revolutionary governments and cultures—even those created by Communism.[16] In keeping with this new spirit of cultural sensitivity, the Presbyterian Church U.S.A. noted in 1956: "Our sensitivity to the need of peoples is not keeping pace with their rising demand for justice, equality, and brotherhood. . . . Ecumenical mission is the whole Church in the whole world releasing its whole life in dynamic mission, with the purpose of entering directly and vitally into an encounter with the world in the name of Jesus Christ. Too long the Church has ignored His command to be one in Him, that the world may believe. In the urgency of our time it dare do so no longer."[17] The missionary arm of the church was beginning to repent of its former alliance with American paternalism and was preparing to operate in a new-found ethos that stressed international partnership.

THE ECUMENICAL EMPHASIS

This growing Presbyterian openness was not limited to cultural issues however. Just as the church became more aware of the political assumptions that underlay its message, so also did it begin to understand its theological provincialism. This awareness developed, in large measure, as a result of Presbyterian involvement in the ecumenical movement. Beginning in 1908, with the formation of the Federal Council of Churches, American Protestants had allied themselves in order to "express the fellowship and Catholic unity of the Christian Church" and "to bring the Christian body of America into united service for Christ and the world." The Federal Council, comprised of thirty-one member denominations by 1910, did not require members to affirm a detailed creed or to adopt any particular form of ecclesiastical government; the sole requirement for membership was the simple affirmation of Jesus Christ as "Divine Lord and Savior."[18]

Although the ecumenical movement had its roots in international dialogue, the first tangible result of postwar ecumenism among American Presbyterians occurred among different Presbyterian denominations within the bounds of the United States. For decades, the several American Presbyterian bodies had considered mergers that would unite regional bodies into one national church. Although the Cumberland Presbyterian Church had successfully united with the Presbyterian Church in the United States of America at the start of the century, unity among the regional bodies seemed elusive, despite repeated merger initiatives. In 1951, however, three-way negotiations between the Presbyterian Church U.S.A., the United Presbyterian Church of North America (the denomination formed from two Scottish-American bodies, the Associate Reformed Church, and the Associate Presbyterian Church), and the Presbyterian Church U.S. began in earnest. Though the Presbyterian Church U.S. would eventually withdraw from the proposed merger (and would not participate in merger negotiations until 1969), these talks led to the formation, in May 1958, of the largest Presbyterian denomination in the nation—the United Presbyterian Church in the United States of America. The new body immediately tended to internal restructuring, one result of which was the formation of the Commission on Ecumenical Mission and Relations (COEMAR). This Commission's broad task was to oversee evangelism, Christian education, interchurch service, and Christian social and welfare services.[19]

In the years following World War II, three other developments stimulated ecumenism beyond the horizons of Presbyterianism: the founding, in 1948, of the World Council of Churches (itself an outgrowth of several other ecumenical movements in which Presbyterians had been involved, including foreign missions, the Y.M.C.A., the Faith and Order movement, and the Life and Work movement), the formation of the National Council of Churches in 1950, and the Consultation on Church Union, begun in 1961.

As involvement with the broader ecumenical movement developed, however, serious theological problems arose among American Presbyterians. What did it mean for Presbyterians, whose unique doctrine and form of government had been carefully articulated over four centuries, to strengthen relations with other denominations? Would such contact somehow dilute

Presbyterian distinctives? This sort of question was raised poignantly during the mid-1960s because of the Consultation on Church Union and in the wake of the sweeping changes proposed during the Roman Catholic Church's formative Second Vatican Council.

The impetus behind the Consultation on Church Union came from a Presbyterian. On 4 December 1960 Eugene Carson Blake,* preaching at Grace Episcopal Cathedral in San Francisco at the invitation of Bishop James A. Pike, called for a union of churches that would be both "truly catholic" and "truly reformed." Blake, stated clerk of the United Presbyterian Church U.S.A., intended that those churches that affirmed the Apostles' and Nicene creed, that observed baptism and the Lord's Supper, and that believed in a continuation of the historic episcopate should find a basis for unity. The following May the Presbyterian General Assembly issued a formal invitation to the Episcopal Church, the Methodist Church, and the United Church of Christ to join in the formation of the Consultation on Church Union. The Presbyterian Church U.S. later joined the discussions.[20]

There is no small significance in the fact that Blake's overture took place one month after the nation had elected its first Roman Catholic president. The religious hegemony once enjoyed by mainline Protestants, Presbyterians included, was eroding. Although the forum produced a measure of cooperation, the Consultation on Church Union would never bring about the full-scale union that Blake had envisioned.

The Roman Catholic Church had resisted involvements in the larger ecumenical movement, but modernizing forces unleashed by Vatican II led to new Catholic attitudes about their old nemesis, Protestantism. Since the Council of Trent in 1545, the Roman communion had viewed Protestants with suspicion and disdain. But now, to the surprise of Christians around the globe, a new form of tolerance prevailed in Rome as Catholic leaders appeared ready to engage other communions in dialogue. For their part, Presbyterians found themselves compelled to develop policies appropriate to the new situation. In 1963, the United Presbyterian Church U.S.A. counseled members to uphold their Presbyterian heritage while remaining open to the Roman ecumenical initiative. Neither Presbyterians nor Catholics, they noted, should seek concessions that required theological compromise. Rather, in a spirit of mutual respect, the two traditions should seek "mutual understanding" in an effort to discover a "more complete comprehension of the obedience to God's truth and its meaning for his Church and the world."[21]

Presbyterianism's new relationships with other ecclesial bodies, despite the considerable interest such encounters engendered, most often were conducted at the denominational level. Though some congregations did engage in local ecumenical dialogue, such endeavors generally fell to local pastors and church leaders from presbyteries, synods, and the assemblies. But the legacy of the 1960s also included issues that were felt more keenly at the local level.

THE STRUGGLE FOR INCLUSION

Throughout the history of American Protestantism, women have generally outnumbered men in church membership. This numerical superiority notwithstanding, women's participation in the churches has been limited to particular spheres of activity and authority. In Presbyterianism, the Sunday school, local missions organizations, and relief societies were envisioned and administered by women, but women were forbidden to participate in roles traditionally viewed as more powerful. Presbyterian women could not be elected deacons, they were not permitted to be ordained as ruling elders or teaching elders, and their participation in the liturgical life of the church was similarly restricted. An effort to open the Presbyterian Church U.S.A. diaconate to women failed in 1890, though that right was afforded Presbyterian women in several other Presbyterian denominations near the turn of the century.

Despite this new access to leadership opportunities, Presbyterian women remained frustrated. The traditional Presbyterian distinctions between deacons, ruling elders, and teaching elders—and the varying degree of authority each office could wield—made access to the diaconate something of a second prize: Although women could serve as deacons they were still denied access to the authority to teach and rule that came with ordination as elders. Indeed, although a Kentucky presbytery of the Cumberland Presbyterian Church ordained Louisa Woosley to the office of elder in 1889, the ordination of women to the full ministry of Word and Sacrament in the northern Presbyterian church was hotly contested until 1921. In that year, the issue was resolved theologically with the decision to include both men and women in the understanding of the term "man" as it was used both in Scripture and in official church documents. In the 1920s, however, agitation increased for women's access to the ordained ministry, in large measure because in 1924 the women's organization was absorbed into a new governing structure that left women virtually powerless within the denomination if they did not have ordained status as elders or clergy. Despite setbacks following World War II, women's ordination was fully affirmed in 1957 during the period in which the predominantly northern United Presbyterian Church was formed, and in 1964 in the largely southern Presbyterian Church in the United States.

By the middle of the turbulent sixties, it appeared, American Presbyterians had been awakened to the unique gifts and ministries of women and to the church's responsibility to acknowledge and affirm these realities. In a comment in 1965, one United Presbyterian Church U.S.A. board noted, "More often than not we have found that the women of the Church are much better prepared than the general constituency to understand the situation abroad and to respond with Christian faith to new challenges."[22]

Although women had often enrolled in Presbyterian theological seminaries in preparation for work as directors of Christian education—an office traditionally dominated by women, though one that did not carry with it the authority of ordination—since the mid-sixties Presbyterian seminaries have witnessed an increasing enrollment of women. These women have chosen theological curricula specifically designed to prepare leaders for ordained pastoral ministry, and despite frequent resistance from congregations that remain suspicious of female ministers, many of these women have entered the ranks of the ordained and practicing Presbyterian clergy.[23] The new spirit of inclusiveness has prompted changes in the liturgical life of local congregations, many of which now use inclusive language in worship and employ gender-neutral nomenclature in reference to God.

At the same time that Presbyterian women sought a hearing, African-American Presbyterians also struggled for recognition and full participation in the tradition. Despite the segregation that was rampant in the churches and notwithstanding the difficulties that attended the merger of the Cumberland Presbyterian Church with the Presbyterian Church U.S.A. in the first decade of the twentieth century, black Presbyterian leaders worked tirelessly to maintain hard-won victories during the first half of the century. Within both the northern and the southern branches of Presbyterianism, African-American Presbyterian leaders such as John M. Gaston, Henry McCrorey, and Frank C. Shirley formed special-purpose organizations designed to counter the stultifying confines of ecclesiastical segregation. The Afro-American Presbyterian Council, founded in 1894, and the American Negro Academy, formed a year earlier, both served as important conduits through which African-American concerns and leadership eventually flowed into the white Presbyterian mainstream.

During the 1950s these racial developments within Presbyterian official hierarchies were paralleled by an increase in racial concerns in American culture at large. As the nightly news tracked the careers of Baptist civil rights leaders such as Martin Luther King, Jr., and followed the formation and efforts of the Southern Christian Leadership Conference, a cadre of black Presbyterians capitalized on new opportunities within the denominations. Both the northern and southern churches instituted Assembly councils on race relations, and in 1963 a group of concerned leaders within the northern church formed the Presbyterian Interracial Council, the body that was instrumental in nominating and electing the first black moderator of the northern General Assembly in 1964, Edler G. Hawkins. This historic development, occurring as it did in the midst of the larger civil rights movement, signaled to the church and to the larger culture as well that racial justice had become and would remain a central concern of the Presbyterian tradition in America. Hawkins's election to the most prestigious post in the church in a decade when, as one board report put it, "men and women listen to the echoes of violence and injustice in our land," was a hopeful sign in a decade fraught with cultural perils.[24]

The Confession of 1967 marked another milestone in the doctrinal life of the church, one that both reflected and made possible many of the liberalizing trends among northern Presbyterians. After the Auburn Affirmation and the subsequent defection of fundamentalists, northern Presbyterians had largely abandoned ef-

forts to arrive at confessional unity; they sought instead, in the words of one
Presbyterian historian, "confessional decentralization." After the merger of the
Presbyterian Church in the U.S.A. and the United Presbyterian Church of North
America in 1958, the first General Assembly of the new denomination appointed
a committee, chaired by Edward A. Dowey, to prepare a "brief contemporary
statement of faith." In 1965 the committee, averring that no one statement could
fully capture the essence of the faith, proposed a *Book of Confessions*, which
included statements of faith from various eras of church history, together with
a new statement, adopted two years later, called the Confession of 1967.[25]

The confession, still reacting to fundamentalist insistence on biblical inerrancy
and reflecting the influence of Neo-orthodoxy over the course of the previous
decades, subordinated the Bible to Christ: "The one sufficient revelation of God
is Jesus Christ, the Word of God incarnate." Acknowledging the importance of
biblical criticism, the confession declared that the Bible should be approached
with "literary and historical understanding" and that its meaning became clear
to the believer only through "the illumination of the Holy Spirit." More important, the confession understood faith as moving beyond mere affirmation to
demonstrate "a present witness to God's grace in Jesus Christ" through a ministry
of reconciliation. The confession even enumerated areas of concern: racial and
ethnic discrimination; the dangers of nationalism; the persistence of poverty
throughout the world; and "anarchy in sexual relationships." Finally, in a controversial passage the confession asserted that the quest for justice and reconciliation required "fresh and responsible relations across every line of conflict,
even at risk to national security."

During the 1960s, then, the Presbyterian traditions in the United States underwent a period of cultural, social, and theological liberalization. The national
bodies, especially in the largely northern United Presbyterian Church U.S.A.,
became increasingly critical of American imperialism, they participated in ecumenical dialogue with Protestants, Catholics, and with members of other religions, and they affirmed the central tenets of the women's movement and the
civil rights movement.

Not everyone greeted these developments with enthusiasm. Korean Presbyterians were generally quite conservative, both theologically and politically. Their
numbers increased dramatically from 1970 to 1990, making them the fastest-
growing constituency within the denomination. Many American Presbyterians,
moreover, especially those who observed these liberal developments from the
comfort of their favorite Sunday morning pew, were troubled by the cultural
and theological shifts that characterized the churches during the 1960s. Many
local congregations believed that national leadership of the churches, esconced
in a complex and burgeoning bureaucracy, was out of touch with the everyday
problems of the annual budget, leaky roofs, the Sunday school, and local membership drives. This concern over the increasingly liberal social and theological
affirmations of the national churches is typified by the complaint sent to the
United Presbyterian Church U.S.A. Assembly by the Presbytery of South Bend,

Indiana, in 1961. Worried over the church's alliance with the National Council of Churches, South Bend argued that although the council could "clarify the issues in particular matters, call for action in areas of need, and lend prayerful support to those forces working for the improvement of the conditions of men," it "should be beyond the bounds of [the Council's] authority and duty to endorse or condemn specific legislative acts, or proposals by organizations, and thereby lend her influence to these measures as if she spoke the unified voice of Protestant Christianity within this land."[26]

If South Bend's expression was typical of a grass-roots reaction to the liberal hierarchies of the churches, so too was the Assembly's response typical of the national church's reaction to conservative members at the congregational level. As noted in the report of the United Presbyterian Church U.S.A. missions board, which helped to reject South Bend's overture, "responsible Christian bodies [like the National Council] may sometimes be compelled under the guidance of the Holy Spirit to 'endorse or condemn certain legislative acts or proposal of organizations.'"[27] These polar responses, one emanating from the local churches, cautious and concerned over the increasing liberalism in the church, the other descending from the church hierarchy, progressive and committed to new ways of construing the Presbyterian witness in the world, were replicated in a series of crises that occurred in the sixties and seventies.[28]

PROTESTS LEFT AND RIGHT

The most notorious of these crises occurred in 1971. Angela Davis, a philosophy professor at the University of California, Los Angeles, a member of the Black Panthers and a self-avowed Communist, had been indicted on conspiracy charges resulting from a violent courtroom incident in San Rafael, California. In an effort to support Davis, the Council on Church and Race of the United Presbyterian Church U.S.A. sent a ten-thousand-dollar contribution to the defense fund set up on Davis's behalf. Individuals throughout the church raised objections to the gift, and in response to these complaints a group of twenty African-American Presbyterians sent the moderator of the United Presbyterian Church U.S.A. a matching gift drawn from their personal funds. This additional support, given with the understanding that it was not to reimburse the church, but to show support for its initial grant to Davis, set in motion a series of debates about the extent to which the church should support political causes of any sort, let alone those involving people whose commitments stood in stark relief to the status quo racial and political sensibilities of the mainline churches.[29]

Nor were the controversies between conservative and liberal Presbyterians limited to intramural debates between local churches and denominational hierarchies. In 1972, after years of debate about the ordination of women, the ownership of local church property, and the extent to which local parishes had to conform to denominational policies, several leading congregations left their mainline denominations to form the Presbyterian Church in America. It was dedicated to the conservation of traditional Presbyterian polity and practice, and gained a foothold within a culture that had swung noticeably to the political and cultural right during the Reagan era. Today the Presbyterian Church in America is one of the fastest-growing of the several smaller Presbyterian bodies in the nation. Though several proposals have surfaced to merge these conservative bodies into a larger, national Presbyterian denomination, concerns over regional strength, ethnic makeup, and particular theological emphases have prevented such a merger among bodies such as the Presbyterian Church in America, the Orthodox Presbyterian Church, and the Associate Reformed Presbyterian Church.

THE MERGER OF 1983

Despite the rifts and realignments that were occurring within the larger Presbyterian tradition in America, the 1960s did see serious negotiations begin between the largest of the mainline Presbyterian bodies in the nation. In 1969 talks began in earnest between representatives of the Presbyterian Church U.S. and the United Presbyterian Church U.S.A. Several major obstacles—regional sensibilities and traditions, theological questions, and problems attending a host of governance questions—stood in the way of merger.

Just two years before the merger negotiations began, the United Presbyterian Church U.S.A. had recast its confessional stance with the compilation of a *Book of Confessions*. Having just formulated the new Confession of 1967, the United Presbyterian Church U.S.A. gathered eight other historic documents into a collection that was to serve as a confessional foundation and guide to the church. Two ancient confessions, the Apostles' Creed and the Nicene Creed, were included, as were three Reformation-era documents, the Scots, the Heidelberg, and the Second Helvetic Confessions. The Westminster Confession and Shorter Catechism (both of which, with the Larger Catechism, had long been in use in the United Presbyterian Church U.S.A.) were included, as was the more recent Theological Declaration of Barmen.

By contrast, however, the Presbyterian Church U.S. recognized only three documents—the Westminster Confession and both the Shorter and Larger Catechisms. Moreover, by the mid-sixties several governance practices separated the two bodies. The United Presbyterian Church U.S.A., for instance, was far more aggressive in its support of the ordination of women and was hardly prepared to offer up its support of women as a bargaining point in the negotiations.

In 1977, as a symbol of the progress in reunion negotiations, the two bodies decided to convene their respective General Assemblies in the same cities at the same time in alternating years. Representative committees from both denominations hammered out solutions to the host of problems that attended the reunion, and in 1981 and 1982 the presbyteries of each body discussed details of several plans.

Finally, in Atlanta, on 10 June 1983, at the 195th anniversary of the first meeting of an American General Assembly, the two bodies formalized their reunion, and changed the name of the reunited church to the Presbyterian Church (U.S.A.). The Larger Catechism was added to the *Book of Confessions*, which became the doctrinal standard for the church, and a committee was formed to draft a new brief statement of Reformed faith for the new church. After more than a century of separation, the new denomination, comprised of some thirteen thousand congregations and more than three million members, was once again a truly national church.

PRESBYTERIANS AND THE POSTMODERN CHALLENGE

In a provocative essay written in 1981, Professor Langdon Gilkey of the University of Chicago outlined the dilemmas that face most mainline denominations in the closing decades of the twentieth century.[30] Describing what many have called the challenge of the postmodern or "post–Enlightenment" era, Gilkey reasoned that the position of traditional Christianity in the contemporary world is increasingly ambiguous. The Enlightenment, itself a cultural ethos in which the American churches prospered and on which they relied, has not delivered on its claim to reduce suffering through technological progress. Some members of the human family have access to advanced medical technologies, but most do not. All of humanity has learned to live in fear of technologies— not least of which is the nuclear threat—whose express purpose is the destruction of human life. Nor, in Gilkey's opinion, has the Enlightenment's quest for individual freedom and democratic structures ended in success.

This century has witnessed social and national tensions, both within and between individual nations, that have issued in massive violence, oppression, and destruction. Despite recent rapprochements between the superpowers that have ended the Cold War, the world community is busy restructuring military systems in order to wage conventional war. Christianity itself has become but one voice in a larger worldwide religious conversation. No longer does Christian faith, despite its several worldviews in distinct national, ethnic, and denominational communities, hold sway over the religions of the world. Hinduism, Buddhism, Islam, and several variants of secularism and communism, all with unique understandings of human meaning, are increasingly ascendent in the world, and they challenge Christianity's historic exclusivism and apparent predominance.

As pessimistic as these findings may be—at the end of his essay Gilkey confesses that he finds the situation akin to being on a sea with no maps—the cultural realities that Gilkey identifies combine to form a clear and distinct challenge to the continued existence of all of America's traditional denominations. Like its Christian partners in mission to the world, the American Presbyterian tradition is subject to the difficulties and ambiguities that will surround organized Christianity as it moves into the twenty-first century. It remains to be seen how the tradition will handle these challenges. How, for instance, will

American Presbyterians respond to the end of the Cold War? More important perhaps, how will they respond to ever-shifting cultural norms? Early in 1991 a special task force on human sexuality for the Presbyterian Church (U.S.A.) issued a report that, among other recommendations, lent its support to sexual relations between people of the same gender and to sexual relations outside of marriage. Presbyterians around the country ordered over forty thousand copies of the report, which received coverage in the media. Delegates to the General Assembly, meeting in Baltimore, overwhelmingly rejected the report and approved a pastoral letter upholding traditional Christian views of sexuality. "We have strongly affirmed the sanctity of the marriage covenant between one man and one woman," the letter declared, "to be a God-given relationship to be honored by marital fidelity."

Does the action of the 1991 General Assembly portend a conservative swing for American Presbyterians? Faced with a massive loss of members since 1965 and a general sense (despite conflicting and inconclusive evidence) that the more conservative, evangelical churches have benefited from the Presbyterians' decline, a move toward the right holds undeniable appeal. Indeed, if success is reckoned in numbers, the most successful religious traditions in American history have purveyed a simple, rather unambiguous message—Methodists during the nineteenth century, the Baptists, the Mormons, twentieth-century evangelicals. Twentieth-century Presbyterians, however, with their embrace of both racial and gender inclusivity and their insistence that a vibrant faith must address the contemporary world in a relevant way, hold to a theology that, at times, is necessarily fraught with ambiguity. The price of fidelity to such standards may well be that American Presbyterianism will never again approach the level of numerical strength or cultural dominance that it enjoyed in the immediate postwar era.

If Gilkey is correct, the long-term survival of mainline Protestantism, including the Presbyterians, will require more than mere theological adjustment, especially at a time when confessional distinctions have blurred and denominations themselves have become increasingly irrelevant. Many Presbyterians may find it uncomfortable to be cast adrift in a sea with no maps, but the Presbyterian tradition in America has a wealth of history and faith on which to draw as it seeks to engage the new world that is emerging. Its faith in a great, sovereign God who is both transcendent over creation and yet intimately, personally involved in the life of that creation; its commitment to representative ecclesial government; its ongoing struggle for a united witness of word, deed, and sacrament; its attempts to bring about genuine institutional harmony in the face of cultural and social diversity—all these facets of the Presbyterian tradition should serve, as they have in the past, as guideposts as the tradition faces an uncertain future.

NOTES

1. During most of the nineteenth century Presbyterianism was American Protestantism's third largest denominational family; only the Methodist and Baptist traditions had

greater total memberships. Just after the opening of the twentieth century, Presbyterian membership fell to fourth position, after being surpassed by the American Lutheran churches. About 1975, the Disciples of Christ tradition took over the fourth position, and the Presbyterians fell to fifth. Presbyterians were not the only American Protestants to face declining membership in the decade of the 1960s. For a comparison of membership statistics within the various branches of Protestantism in the era, see Edwin S. Gaustad, *Historical Atlas of Religion in America*, rev. ed. (New York: Harper & Row, 1976).

2. One of the best sources for study of American Protestantism after World War II is Robert Wuthnow, *The Restructuring of American Religion: Society and Faith Since World War II* (Princeton, N.J.: Princeton University Press, 1988). Wuthnow has given particular attention to the Presbyterian tradition in this period in his essay "The Restructuring of American Presbyterianism: Turmoil in One Denomination," in *The Presbyterian Predicament: Six Perspectives* ed. Milton J. Coalter, John M. Mulder, and Louis B. Weeks (Louisville, Ky.: Westminster/John Knox Press, 1990), pp. 27–48.

3. Sydney E. Ahlstrom, *A Religious History of the American People* (New Haven, Conn.: Yale University Press, 1972), p. 1079.

4. The bibliographic data for the various collections of *Minutes* through the early seventies is as follows: *Minutes of General Assembly of The Presbyterian Church in the U.S.A.* (Philadelphia: Office of the General Assembly, 1945–1957) [hereafter noted as "PCUSA" followed by the year of publication and the page number]; *Minutes of the General Assembly of The United Presbyterian Church in the United States of America* (New York: Office of the General Assembly, 1957–1972) [hereafter noted as "UPCUSA" followed by the year of publication and the page number]; *Minutes of the Presbyterian Church in the United States* (Richmond, Va.: Presbyterian Commission of Publications, 1945–1951; Atlanta: Office of the General Assembly in Atlanta, 1952–1972) [hereafter noted as "PCUS" followed by the year of publication and the page number].

5. PCUS, 1948, 74.

6. PCUSA, 1952, 177.

7. PCUSA, 1952, 178.

8. PCUSA, 1952, 178.

9. UPCUSA, 1960, 205.

10. UPCUSA, 1960, 202.

11. Military statistics on the Vietnam War are available in Harry G. Summers, Jr., *Vietnam War Almanac* (New York: Facts on File Publications, 1985).

12. UPCUSA, 1964, 259–260.

13. See The Layman's Foreign Missions Inquiry, The Commission of Appraisal, William Ernest Hocking, chairman, *Re-Thinking Missions: A Laymen's Inquiry After One Hundred Years* (New York: Harper & Brothers, 1932). For a detailed account of the changes that affected the Presbyterian foreign missions enterprise in the twentieth century, see John R. Fitzmier and Randall Balmer, "A Poultice for the Bite of the Cobra: The Hocking Report and Presbyterian Missions in the Middle Decades of the Twentieth Century," in *The Diversity of Discipleship: The Presbyterians and Twentieth-Century Christian Witness*, ed. Milton J. Coalter, John M. Mulder, and Louis B. Weeks (Louisville, Ky.: Westminster/John Knox Press, 1991), pp. 105–125.

14. PCUSA, 1947, 172, 174.

15. PCUS, 1945, 80.

16. PCUSA, 1955, 158–159.

17. PCUSA, 1956, 170–171. Ellipsis in original.

18. For a full history of the worldwide ecumenical movement, see Ruth Rouse and

Stephen Charles Neill, eds., *A History of the Ecumenical Movement, 1517–1948*, 2d ed. (London: SPCK, 1967); and Harold E. Fey, ed., *The Ecumenical Advance: A History of the Ecumenical Movement, Volume 2, 1948–1968* (London: SPCK, 1970). The quotations appear in Rouse and Neill, *History of the Ecumenical Movement*, p. 621.

19. See PCUSA, 1957, 177.

20. See Erskine Clarke, "Presbyterian Ecumenical Activity in the United States," in *Diversity of Discipleship*, ed., Coalter, Mulder, and Weeks, pp. 149–69.

21. UPCUSA, 1963, 290.

22. UPCUSA, 1965, 265.

23. See Barbara Brown Zikmund, "Ministry of Word and Sacrament: Women and Changing Understandings of Ordination," in *Presbyterian Predicament*, ed. Coalter, Mulder, and Weeks, pp. 134–158.

24. UPCUSA, 1963, 280; See Gayraud S. Wilmore, "Identity and Integration: Black Presbyterians and Their Allies in the Twentieth Century" in *Presbyterian Predicament* ed. Coalter, Mulder, and Weeks, pp. 109–133.

25. This discussion is indebted to James H. Moorhead, "Redefining Confessionalism: American Presbyterians in the Twentieth Century," in *The Confessional Mosaic: Presbyterians and Twentieth-Century Theology*, ed. Milton J. Coalter, John M. Mulder, and Louis B. Weeks (Louisville, Ky.: Westminster/John Knox Press, 1990), pp. 59–83.

26. UPCUSA, 1962, 29. This Overture appears in a section of the *Minutes* titled "General Assembly Documents." It is of some interest to note here the parallels that exist to the controversies surrounding the "spirituality of the church" that were so prominent among American Presbyterians during the nineteenth century.

27. UPCUSA, 1962, 315.

28. For detailed analyses of these problems see Dean R. Hoge, *Division in the Protestant House: The Basic Reasons Behind Intra-Church Conflicts* (Philadelphia: Westminster Press, 1976); and Wuthnow, "The Restructuring of American Presbyterianism: Turmoil in One Denomination," in *Presbyterian Predicament*, ed. Coalter, Mulder, and Weeks, pp. 27–48.

29. For a detailed analysis of the Davis affair see Hoge, p. 106 ff.

30. Langdon Gilkey, "The New Watershed in Theology," *Soundings* 64 (1981): 118–131.

A CHRONOLOGY
OF AMERICAN
PRESBYTERIANISM

1643 British Parliament convenes the Westminster Assembly. *The Form of Presbyterial Church Government*, *The Directory of Public Worship*, *The Westminster Confession of Faith*, *The Larger Catechism*, and *The Shorter Catechism* are published in the ensuing years.

1667 Presbyterian congregation is organized in Newark, New Jersey; congregations subsequently founded in Elizabeth, New Jersey (1668); Woodbridge, New Jersey (1680); Fairfield, Connecticut (1692); and Philadelphia (1692).

1706 Francis Makemie and seven other ministers form the first American presbytery.

1716 First American Presbyterian Synod is organized in Philadelphia.

1720 Theodore Frelinghuysen, a product of Reformed pietism in the Old World, comes to the Raritan Valley.

1727 William Tennent, Sr., moves to Neshaminy, Pennsylvania, and begins his Log College.

1729 The Adopting Act of 1729, crafted primarily by Jonathan Dickinson, seeks to distinguish between essential and nonessential components of the Westminster standards.

1736 The subscriptionist–antirevival coalition effectively rescinds the Adopting Act of 1729 and imposes strict subscription on all members of the Synod.

1738 The New Light party, headed by Gilbert Tennent, establishes the New Brunswick Presbytery.

1740 Gilbert Tennent preaches his famous *The Danger of an Unconverted Ministry* at Nottingham, Pennsylvania.

1741 Schism occurs between New Side and Old Side Presbyterians over the legitimacy of the Great Awakening.

1743 Francis Alison establishes the New London Academy.

1745 The New York Presbytery, under the leadership of Jonathan Dickinson, withdraws from the Synod of Philadelphia and, with the revival party, forms the Synod of New York.

1746 John Hamilton, interim governor of New Jersey, signs a charter for the College of New Jersey; classes begin in Elizabethtown, New Jersey, the following year.

1752 Samuel Davies' appeal to the Bishop of London is designed to secure religious liberty for Virginia Presbyterians.

1758 Old Side and New Side Presbyterians reunite.

1766 John Witherspoon is chosen president of Princeton; he assumes his post in 1768.

1779 Thomas Jefferson introduces his "Bill for Establishing Religious Freedom"; finally enacted in Virginia in 1786.

1782 Reformed and Associate Presbyteries unite to form the Associate Reformed Presbyterian Church.

1785 James Madison writes "Memorial and Remonstrance."

1786 Synod selects a special committee to draft a Plan of Government with a view toward a national church.

1789 First General Assembly of the Presbyterian Church in the United States of America (PCUSA) is held in Philadelphia. The Assembly extends over four synods—New York and New Jersey, Philadelphia, Virginia, and the Carolinas.

1801 The Cane Ridge revival is held in Kentucky. The Plan of Union is adopted, uniting Presbyterians and Congregationalists. The PCUSA General Assembly appoints John Chavis first Presbyterian missionary to African-American slaves.

1804 Barton Stone and his followers withdraw from the PCUSA and later join Alexander Campbell's "Christian" denomination.

1807 Archibald Alexander forms the Presbyterian Evangelical Society of Philadelphia.

1807 First African Presbyterian Church is begun under John Gloucester.

1810 Samuel McAdow, Finis Ewing, and Samuel King form an independent presbytery, forerunner of the Cumberland Presbyterian Church.

1822 African-American Presbyterians establish congregations in New York City (1822); Reading, Pennsylvania (1823); Newark, New Jersey (1835); Princeton, New Jersey (1845); Baltimore (1853); the District of Columbia (1841); and Harrisburg, Pennsylvania (1858).

1828 Theodore S. Wright becomes the first African-American graduate of a Presbyterian seminary (Princeton Theological Seminary).

1833 Charles Colcock Jones develops plantation missions in concert with the Association for the Religious Instruction of Negroes.

1837 Old School and New School factions divide at the PCUSA General Assembly; the 1801 Plan of Union declared unconstitutional.

1857 Southern New School Presbyterians form United Synod of the South.

1858 The Associate Reformed Church and the Associate Church unite to form the United Presbyterian Church of North America.

1861 PCUSA General Assembly passes Spring Resolution affirming its support of the Federal Union. Presbyterian Church in the Confederate States of America is formed by southern Old School Presbyterians in Augusta, Georgia.

1864 Presbyterian Church in the Confederate States of America merges with United

Synod of the South to form the Presbyterian Church in the United States (PCUS), whose first General Assembly gathers the following year.

1869 New School and Old School northern bodies reunite.

1871 First Synod of the Colored Cumberland Presbyterian Church is formed.

1892 In response to the controversy raised in the Briggs Trial, the PCUSA General Assembly declares the original manuscripts of the Bible to be "without error."

1901 A. L. Philips and E. W. Williams lead the movement to form the independent Afro-American Presbyterian Synod.

1906 The Cumberland Presbyterian Church and the PCUSA reunite.

1910 The PCUSA General Assembly, concerned about the modernist threat, adopts the "five points" of fundamentalism.

1922 Harry Emerson Fosdick preaches "Shall the Fundamentalists Win?" from the pulpit of First Presbyterian Church in New York City.

1924 The "Auburn Affirmation" is published.

1925 The infamous "Scopes Monkey Trial" is held in Dayton, Tennessee.

1929 The PCUSA General Assembly reorganizes Princeton Theological Seminary; J. Gresham Machen begins the rival Westminster Seminary in Philadelphia.

1930 The Laymen's Foreign Missions Inquiry, with the financial backing of John D. Rockefeller, Jr., begins study of Protestant missions that eventuates in the summary volume, *Re-Thinking Missions*, in 1932.

1936 Machen and fellow conservatives form the independent Presbyterian Church of America that later becomes the Orthodox Presbyterian Church.

1948 The World Council of Churches is formed.

1950 The National Council of Churches is formed.

1956 PCUSA affirms the ordination of women.

1958 The United Presbyterian Church in North America and the PCUSA merge to form the United Presbyterian Church in the United States of America (UPCUSA).

1961 Consultation on Church Union is begun.

1964 PCUS affirms the ordination of women. Edler G. Hawkins becomes the first African-American elected moderator of the UPCUSA General Assembly.

1967 The UPCUSA Confession of 1967 and the *Book of Confessions* are published.

1972 Conservatives withdraw from the PCUS to form the Presbyterian Church in America.

1983 UPCUSA and the PCUS reunite to form the Presbyterian Church, U.S.A. This historic event ends the century-long division of the America's largest Presbyterian bodies.

BIBLIOGRAPHIC ESSAY

The following essay is intended as a guide to further reading and research in American Presbyterian history. The essay is divided into several sections, each of which treats a particular era or topic in the development of Presbyterianism in America. Although it is not an exhaustive survey of historical writing about American Presbyterianism, it is sufficiently detailed to allow the general reader access to the more specialized scholarly work that informs the present volume.

GENERAL RESOURCES FOR THE STUDY OF AMERICAN PRESBYTERIAN HISTORY

Although the American Presbyterian experience has generated a rich specialized literature, students of the tradition may find it best to begin their study of the Presbyterians with one of several narrative texts that offer overviews of the history of religion in America. Fortunately, there are several fine studies from which to choose, and some of these have been revised and updated to keep abreast of current scholarship. Students with particular interest in the history of Protestant thought in America—and particularly its Puritan and Reformed expressions—will find Sydney E. Ahlstrom, *A Religious History of the American People* (New Haven: Yale University Press, 1972) both comprehensive and detailed. Two other narrative texts, both of which have been recently revised, are Winthrop S. Hudson, *Religion in America: An Historical Account of the Development of American Religious Life*, 4th ed. (New York: Macmillan, 1987), and Edwin S. Gaustad, *A Religious History of America*, new rev. ed. (San Francisco: Harper & Row, 1990). While the strength of Ahlstrom's work lies in its lucid exposition of the intellectual and theological currents that run through American Protestant history, the works of both Hudson and Gaustad have the virtue of attention to the diversity within American religion. In addition to the history of Protestant developments that are so keenly elucidated in Ahlstrom, Hudson and Gaustad give greater attention to African-American religion, the religious experience of American women, Catholicism, popular religious themes in American culture, and Eastern religions in America. Students of American Presbyterianism, therefore, will likely want to consult these texts selectively using Ahlstrom to examine the theological backgrounds of Presbyterianism in America, and Hudson and Gaustad to examine the larger social, political, and denominational contexts in which American Presbyterianism developed.

In addition to having published a fine narrative text, Gaustad has also compiled several other resources for the study of religion in America in general, and for the study of American Presbyterianism in particular. The narrative interpretations noted above rest on their respective authors' work in primary sources, edited collections of which can be particularly useful to students of American religion. Gaustad's edited collection, *A Documentary History of Religion in America*, 2 vols. (Grand Rapids, Mich.: William B. Eerdmans, 1982–83), offers a multitude of religious voices—some Presbyterian, some not—that help to place American Presbyterianism in context. Gaustad's other major work—the only volume of its kind—is his *Historical Atlas of Religion in America*, rev. ed. (New York: Harper & Row, 1976), which tracks the development of religious groups in America by denomination, size, growth over time, and region of the nation. Its numerous maps, charts, statistics, and ample commentary make it an invaluable reference for the study of Presbyterianism in America.

A good deal of the best information on American Presbyterianism can be found in articles published in scholarly journals and in collections of edited essays. One journal, solely committed to the publication of Presbyterian historical work, is published by the Presbyterian Historical Society in Philadelphia. Currently entitled *American Presbyterianism*, this fine reference source for focused work on Presbyterian history was formerly published under the title *Journal of Presbyterian History*. Guides to published essays on Presbyterianism are readily available. A general introduction to published work in American religion that is sensitive to Presbyterian issues is Nelson Rollin Burr, *A Critical Bibliography of Religion in America* (Princeton, N.J.: Princeton University Press, 1961); for work in the colonial period, see Leonard J. Trinterud, *A Bibliography of American Presbyterianism During the Colonial Period* (Philadelphia: Presbyterian Historical Society, 1968); a more contemporary and focused bibliography is Harold M. Parker, Jr., comp., *Bibliography of Published Articles on American Presbyterianism, 1901–1980* (Westport, Conn.: Greenwood Press, 1985). Less conventional sources for the study of American Presbyterianism might include the following: Mary H. Plummer, and Gerald W. Gillette, eds., *On Holy Ground—American Presbyterian/Reformed Historical Sites* (Philadelphia: Presbyterian Historical Society, 1982); and James H. Smylie, "American Presbyterians: A Pictorial History," *Journal of Presbyterian History*, 63 (Spring/Summer 1985).

Presbyterians have often written about themselves, and narrative histories of the tradition written by insiders, though sometimes evidencing partisan judgments, remain a useful source of information. Ray A. King, *A History of the Associate Reformed Presbyterian Church* (Charlotte, N.C.: Board of Christian Education of the Associate Reformed Presbyterian Church, 1966), and Ben M. Barrus, Milton L. Baughn, and Thomas H. Campbell, *A People Called Cumberland Presbyterians* (Memphis: Frontier Press, 1972) trace the development of smaller Presbyterian bodies. Lefferts A. Loetscher, *A Brief History of the Presbyterians*, 3d ed. (Philadelphia: Westminster Press, 1978), offers a more comprehensive account of American Presbyterianism; a popular, general account, it remains one of the most useful books of this genre.

Reference works that treat biographical and denominational subjects in American religion abound. Some of the most useful of these collections are: William B. Sprague, ed., *Annals of the American Pulpit*, 9 vols. (New York: Carters, 1857–69; 1969); Allen

Johnson and Dumas Malone, eds., *Dictionary of American Biography*, 20 vols. (New York: Scribner's, 1928–37; Eight Supplements, 1944–88); Henry Warner Bowden, *Dictionary of American Religious Biography* (Westport, Conn.: Greenwood Press, 1977); Daniel G. Reid, Robert D. Linder, Bruce L. Shelley, and Harry S. Stout, eds., *Dictionary of Christianity in America* (Downers Grove: InterVarsity Press, 1990); and Edward T. James et al., eds., *Notable American Women, 1607–1950: A Biographical Dictionary*, 3 vols. (Cambridge: Belknap Press of Harvard University Press, 1971). The intrepid student of the history of the Presbyterian tradition in America may find it necessary to review the official proceedings of the denominations, particularly as recorded in the minutes of the General Assemblies. Records of the smaller, regional bodies are often located in seminary or university libraries, or at denominational libraries or headquarters. The records of the larger bodies are more easily located, and entitled as follows: *Minutes of General Assembly of The Presbyterian Church in the U.S.A.* (Philadelphia: Office of the General Assembly, 1934), and *Minutes of the Presbyterian Church in the United States* (Richmond: Presbyterian Commission of Publications, 1935).

EUROPEAN ORIGINS OF AMERICAN PRESBYTERIANISM

American Presbyterianism's roots lay in the Europe of the Reformation era. Any examination of those roots should consider both the social and intellectual background of the period as well as the specific religious issues that led to the development of Reformed theology in the sixteenth century. Steven Ozment, *The Age of Reform, 1250–1550: An Intellectual and Religious History of Late Medieval and Reformation Europe* (New Haven, Conn.: Yale University Press, 1980), provides a helpful examination of the broader intellectual background of the Reformation era. One of the most helpful introductions to the theological issues that shaped Reformed theology can be found in John T. McNeill, *The History and Character of Calvinism* (New York: Oxford University Press, 1954), the most comprehensive narrative treatment of the larger tradition to date. Also helpful in this respect are Elsie Anne McKee and Brian G. Armstrong, eds., *Probing the Reformed Tradition: Historical Studies in Honor of Edward A. Dowey, Jr.* (Louisville: Westminster/John Knox Press, 1989), and Donald K. McKim, ed., *Encyclopedia of the Reformed Faith* (Louisville: Westminster/John Knox Press, 1992). Interest in particular geographic, national, or ethnic versions of the Calvinist tradition can be pursued in the essays found in W. Stanford Reid, ed., *Probing the Reformed Tradition: Historical Studies in Honor of Edward A. Dowey, Jr.* (Louisville: Westminster/John Knox Press, 1989), and Donald K. McKim, ed., *Encyclopedia of the Reformed Faith* (Louisville: Westminster/John Knox Press, 1992). Interest in particular geographic, national, or ethnic versions of the Calvinist tradition can be pursued in the essays found in W. Stanford Reid, ed., *John Calvin: His Influence in the Western World* (Grand Rapids: Zondervan, 1982). While these two sources treat the tradition broadly, John H. Leith, *An Introduction to the Reformed Tradition: A Way of Being the Christian Community*, rev. ed. (Atlanta: John Knox Press, 1977), provides a helpful account of the particular ecclesiastical issues that informed the development of the tradition.

Our understanding of the Reformed branch of Reformation theology has been shaped by the work of generations of scholars who have given particular attention to the tradition's founders and leaders, particularly Calvin, Zwingli, Bullinger, and Knox. Although older—and often appreciative—treatments of Calvin, such as Williston Walker, *John Calvin: The Organiser of Reformed Protestantism, 1509—1564* (New York: G. P. Putnam

& Sons, 1906), continue to find an audience, several more recent examinations of Calvin have changed the manner in which he is viewed. Two volumes that fall into this latter category are T.H.L. Parker, *John Calvin: A Biography* (Philadelphia: Westminster Press, 1975), and, more recently, William James Bouwsma, *John Calvin: A Sixteenth-Century Portrait* (New York: Oxford University Press, 1988). For an overview of Calvin's theology, see François Wendel, *Calvin: The Origins and Development of his Religious Thought*, trans. Philip Mairet (New York: Harper & Row, 1963). A good deal of the reflection on Calvin's thought, if not his larger intellectual life, is based on his biblical commentaries and his monumental *Institutes*. Calvin's exegetical work can be seen in *Calvin's Commentaries*, trans. and ed. by Joseph Haroutunian, in collaboration with Louise Pettibone Smith, *The Library of Christian Classics*, vol. 23 (Philadelphia: Westminster Press, 1958). The recognized critical scholarly edition of Calvin's *Institutes* in English is John Calvin, *Institutes of the Christian Religion*, 2 vols., ed. John T. McNeill, trans. Ford Lewis Battles, *The Library of Christian Classics*, vols. 20 and 21 (Philadelphia: Westminster Press, 1960).

Calvin was hardly the only shaper of Reformed thought: Ulrich Zwingli, Heinrich Bullinger, Theodore Beza, and a host of English theologians also exerted enormous influence on the tradition. Zwingli's life is examined in George Richard Potter, *Zwingli* (New York: Cambridge University Press, 1976); a recent helpful work on his theology is W. P. Stephens, *The Theology of Huldrych Zwingli* (New York: Oxford University Press, 1986). For an examination of Bullinger's theology and his relationship to the larger Reformed tradition, see J. Wayne Baker, *Heinrich Bullinger and the Covenant: The Other Reformed Tradition* (Athens: Ohio University Press, 1980); on Knox, see Jasper Godwin Ridley, *John Knox* (New York: Oxford University Press, 1968).

As the first chapter of the present volume has tried to convey, the Reformed tradition is not monolithic. Rather, it exhibits a degree of internal diversity which has led to the development of distinct sub-groups that have competed for recognition. Over the last several decades scholars have offered a number of helpful studies that treat topics about which reformed theologians have disagreed. On predestination see, for instance, Richard A. Muller, *Christ and the Decree: Christology and Predestination in Reformed Theology from Calvin to Perkins* (Durham, N.C.: Labyrinth Press, 1986); on federal theology, David A. Weir, *The Origins of Federal Theology in Sixteenth-Century Reformation Thought* (New York: Oxford University Press, 1990); and on Arminianism, Carl Oliver Bangs, *Arminius: A Study in the Dutch Reformation* (Nashville: Abingdon Press, 1971); and Richard A. Muller, *God, Creation, and Providence in the Thought of Jacob Arminius: Sources and Directions of Scholastic Protestantism in the Era of Early Orthodoxy* (Grand Rapids: Baker Book House, 1991). These internecine squabbles have led some scholars to question the utility of the expression "Calvinist." Given the internal diversity of the movement and the recognition of several indigenous forms of Reformed theology, the attempt to identify a coherent and consistent trajectory of thought from Calvin to his heirs is problematic. A pointed example of this line of interpretation is found in R. T. Kendall, *Calvin and English Calvinism to 1649* (New York: Oxford University Press, 1979). For a vigorous critique of the Kendall thesis, see Paul Helm, *Calvin and the Calvinists* (Edinburg and Carlisle, Penn.: Banner of Truth, 1982). The entire issue of the *Evangelical Quarterly* 55:2 (1983) is devoted to an examination of the issues standing behind the Kendall-Helm debate.

Many of Calvin's works have been translated into English, but scholars have not produced critical English editions of the work of many other European Reformers. Hence, it is often quite difficult for the beginning student of Reformed theology to locate the primary sources. Although they are arranged topically and sometimes provide only snippets of the original documents, two sources are particularly helpful in providing primary-source documentation of the Reformed tradition in the sixteenth and seventeenth centuries: Heinrich Heppe, *Reformed Dogmatics Set Out and Illustrated from the Sources*, trans. G. T. Thomson, revised and edited by Ernst Bizer (London: George Allen & Unwin, 1956); and John W. Beardslee III, ed., *Reformed Dogmatics: Seventeenth-Century Reformed Theology Through the Writings of Wollebius, Voetius, and Turretin* (New York: Oxford University Press, 1965).

Although the story of the Puritan migration to New England in the 1630s is not directly connected to the birth of the Presbyterian tradition in America, the literature of English and American Puritanism does provide a helpful backdrop to the study of American Presbyterianism. For sustained historical accounts of the relationship between Puritans and Presbyterians in England, the work of Patrick Collinson is particularly helpful; see Collinson, *The Elizabethan Puritan Movement* (Berkeley and Los Angeles: University of California Press, 1967); *The Religion of Protestants: The Church in English Society, 1559–1625* (Oxford: Clarendon Press, 1982); and *Godly People: Essays on English Protestantism and Puritanism* (London: Hambledon Press, 1983). For a treatment of English Presbyterianism, see Peter Lake, *Anglicans and Puritans?: Presbyterianism and English Conformist Thought from Whitgift to Hooker* (London: Allen and Unwin, 1988).

The secondary literature on Puritanism in New England is extraordinarily complex and rich. Several works treat the British and Continental theological backgrounds of American Puritanism and thereby serve as helpful ancillary sources for Presbyterianism in America. Perry Miller, *The New England Mind: The Seventeenth Century* (New York: Macmillan, 1939) remains one of the best overall studies of the movement. Charles L. Cohen, *God's Caress: The Psychology of Puritan Religious Experience* (New York: Oxford University Press, 1986) provides an excellent description of Puritan spirituality. Theodore Dwight Bozeman, *To Live Ancient Lives: The Primitivist Dimension in Puritanism* (Chapel Hill: University of North Carolina Press, 1988) explores the Puritan's interests in recapturing "primitive" New Testament models of church government and piety.

THE COLONIAL AND EARLY NATIONAL EXPERIENCE

The origins of American Presbyterianism, anchored in the Middle Colonies, have only recently begun to attract the attention they deserve, having been eclipsed by the historiographical shadow of New England Puritanism. Ned C. Landsman's study, *Scotland and Its First American Colony* (Princeton, N.J.: Princeton University Press, 1985), offers a transatlantic perspective on Scottish life, culture, and religion. Landsman traces the reasons for the migration, explains the settlement patterns in east New Jersey, and argues that revivalism was essential to the maintenance of the Scottish, particularly in the New World. Leigh Eric Schmidt, *Holy Fairs: Scottish Communions and American Revivals in the Early Modern Period* (Princeton, N.J.: Princeton University Press, 1989), advances the religious component of the equation considerably by arguing that the Scottish practice of sacramental seasons, a protracted observation of the Lord's Supper, came with the Scots to the New World and provided the model for the frontier camp meeting at the turn of the nineteenth century. Marilyn J. Westerkamp also explores the connections between Scots-Irish and American piety, albeit less imaginatively, in *Triumph of the*

Laity: Scots-Irish Piety and the Great Awakening, 1625–1760 (New York: Oxford University Press, 1988).

The standard account of Presbyterianism in the colonial era remains Leonard J. Trinterud, *The Forming of an American Tradition: A Re-examination of Colonial Presbyterianism* (Philadelphia: Westminster Press, 1949). Trinterud takes a decidedly whiggish approach to colonial Presbyterianism, one that occasionally crosses the line into providential history. He sees the hand of God directing a church with, in his words, a "divinely directed mission in American history." Trinterud celebrates the Great Awakening and the triumph of New Light revivalism. The so-called Great Awakening, however, has itself been reexamined since the publication of Trinterud's book. Jon Butler's essay, "Enthusiasm Described and Decried: The Great Awakening as Interpretive Fiction," *Journal of American History*, 69 (1982–1983):305–325, calls into question whether or not such a phenomenon actually occurred or whether what historians refer to as the Great Awakening was in fact merely a series of discrete revivals.

Despite Butler's misgivings, the moniker "Great Awakening" endures, even if it is merely a historical convention. Presbyterianism's role in the Awakening is treated in numerous works, including many of those cited above. Presbyterianism's most conspicuous player in the revival was Gilbert Tennent, whose most recent biography is Milton J. Coalter, Jr., *Gilbert Tennent, Son of Thunder: A Case Study of Continental Pietism's Impact on the First Great Awakening in the Middle Colonies* (Westport, Conn.: Greenwood Press, 1986). Coalter shows Tennent's development into a New Light preacher, influenced both by his father and by Theodorus Jacobus Frelinghuysen, the Dutch pietist who served churches along the Raritan Valley. Randall Balmer examines the critical interplay of Dutch pietism and New Light Presbyterianism in *A Perfect Babel of Confusion: Dutch Religion and English Culture in the Middle Colonies* (New York: Oxford University Press, 1989), and a more general treatment of Presbyterianism in the context of eighteenth-century religious and political life appears in Patricia U. Bonomi, *Under the Cope of Heaven: Religion, Society, and Politics in Colonial America* (New York: Oxford University Press, 1986).

One of the most important consequences of the Great Awakening was the formation of educational institutions throughout the American colonies. Presbyterian opponents of the revival tried to establish their own school (see George Morgan, "The Colonial Origin of Newark Academy," *Delaware Notes*, 8 [1934]:7–30; George H. Ryden, "The Newark Academy of Delaware in Colonial Days," *Pennsylvania History*, 2 [October 1935]:205–224), but the New Lights formed a more important and enduring institution, the College of New Jersey. Alison B. Olson looks at the complex interplay of piety and politics in "The Founding of Princeton University: Religion and Politics in Eighteenth-Century New Jersey," *New Jersey History*, 87 (1969):133–150. Princeton's larger history as an institution appears in Thomas Jefferson Wertenbaker, *Princeton: 1746–1896* (Princeton, N.J.: Princeton University Press, 1946). The considerable contributions of Princeton alumni to the religious, intellectual, and political life of the emerging nation can be traced in several biographical volumes: James McLachlan, Richard A. Harrison, and John M. Murrin, *Princetonians: A Biographical Dictionary*, 4 vols. (Princeton, N.J.: Princeton University Press, 1976–), and, more selectively, in Willard Thorp, ed., *The Lives of Eighteen from Princeton* (Princeton, N.J.: Princeton University Press, 1946).

On the role of Presbyterianism in the American Revolution, two entire fascicles of the *Journal of Presbyterian History* are especially helpful: "Presbyterians and the American Revolution: A Documentary Account," 52 (Winter 1974), and "Presbyterians and the

American Revolution: An Interpretive Account,'' 54 (Spring 1976). Of all the eighteenth-century Presbyterian leaders, none was more influential in the life of the new nation than John Witherspoon. For a biography of the Princeton president who played such an important role in the quest for independence, see Varnum Lansing Collins, *President Witherspoon: A Biography*, 2 vols. (Princeton, N.J.: Princeton University Press, 1925). Mark A. Noll offers a much more nuanced understanding of Witherspoon as well as Princeton's almost symbiotic relationship with political and cultural currents at the turn of the nineteenth century in *Princeton and the Republic, 1768–1822* (Princeton, N.J.: Princeton University Press, 1989).

Presbyterian historians often celebrate what they see as the affinities between Presbyterianism and American culture, some even going so far as to suggest that disestablishment and the American form of government adopted by the founders was indebted to Presbyterian theory and polity. Such enthusiasm should be tempered, however, by the closer examinations provided by Leonard W. Levy, *The Establishment Clause: Religion and the First Amendment* (New York: Macmillan, 1986); Thomas J. Curry, *The First Freedoms: Church and State in America to the Passage of the First Amendment* (New York: Oxford University Press, 1986); and Richard W. Pointer, *Protestant Pluralism and the New York Experience: A Study of Eighteenth-Century Religious Diversity* (Bloomington and Indianapolis: Indiana University Press, 1988).

THE NINETEENTH CENTURY

The antebellum period in American religious historiography is only now beginning to flourish, with the recent publication of several important works. These include Jon Butler, *Awash in a Sea of Faith: Christianizing of the American People* (Cambridge, Mass.: Harvard University Press, 1990), which argues that institutional Christianity began gradually to displace folk religious practice during this period; Nathan O. Hatch, *The Democratization of American Christianity* (New Haven: Yale University Press, 1989), which demonstrates the populist, democratic tendencies of antebellum Protestantism; and Richard T. Hughes and C. Leonard Allen, *Illusions of Innocence: Protestant Primitivism in America, 1630–1875* (Chicago: University of Chicago Press, 1988), which argues that the search for the primordial has been a consistent strain in American religious life.

The Second Great Awakening both drew upon Presbyterian practices (Schmidt, *Holy Fairs*) and dramatically convulsed American Presbyterianism. In the Cumberland Valley, Presbyterian revivalists joined forces with others to shape evangelical culture in the South, the most visible manifestation of which was the camp meeting. For a general history of the Cumberland revival, see John B. Boles, *The Great Revival, 1787–1805* (Lexington: University Press of Kentucky, 1972), and Dickson D. Bruce, Jr., *And They All Sang Hallelujah: Plain-Folk Camp-Meeting Religion, 1800–1845* (Knoxville: University of Tennessee Press, 1974). The Cane Ridge revival (Paul K. Conkin, *Cane Ridge: America's Pentecost* [Madison: University of Wisconsin Press, 1990]), arguably the most spectacular in American history, set the standard for camp-meeting revivals, and, as Donald G. Mathews shows in *Religion in the Old South* (Chicago: University of Chicago Press, 1977), evangelical revivalism left its indelible imprint on southern culture.

The upstate New York theater of the Second Awakening affected American Presbyterianism as well. Charles Grandison Finney's "new measures," as set forth in a modern edition, *Lectures on Revivals of Religion*, ed. William McLoughlin (Cambridge, Mass.: Harvard University Press, 1960), established guidelines for the conduct of revivals. For

Finney and others, the results were dramatic; see Whitney R. Cross, *The Burned-Over District: The Social and Intellectual History of Enthusiastic Religion in Western New York, 1800–1850* (Ithaca, N.Y.: Cornell University Press, 1950); Paul E. Johnson, *A Shopkeeper's Millennium: Society and Revivals in Rochester, New York, 1815–1837* (New York: Hill & Wang, 1978); and Curtis D. Johnson, *Islands of Holiness: Rural Religion in Upstate New York, 1790–1860* (Ithaca, N.Y.: Cornell University Press, 1989). Finney himself still lacks a biographer equal to the task, but the most recent effort is Keith J. Hardman, *Charles Grandison Finney, 1792–1875* (Syracuse, N.Y.: Syracuse University Press, 1987).

The controversy over revivalism split American Presbyterianism in the nineteenth century, just as it had a century earlier; see George M. Marsden, "Perspective on the Division of 1837," in *Pressing Toward the Mark: Essays Commemorating Fifty Years of the Orthodox Presbyterian Church*, ed. Charles G. Dennison and Richard C. Gamble (Philadelphia: Orthodox Presbyterian Church, 1986). Marsden has provided a fuller treatment of this bifurcation in *The Evangelical Mind and the New School Presbyterian Experience: A Case Study of Thought and Theology in Nineteenth-Century America* (New Haven: Yale University Press, 1970). Other studies have examined particular groups or traditions that emerged out of theological and regional divisions within nineteenth-century American Presbyterianism: Harold M. Parker, Jr., *The United Synod of the South: The Southern New School Presbyterian Church* (Westport, Conn.: Greenwood Press, 1988); Louis B. Weeks, *Kentucky Presbyterians* (Atlanta: John Knox Press, 1983); and T. Watson Street, *The Story of Southern Presbyterians* (Richmond: John Knox Press, 1961). By far the most important and comprehensive study of Southern Presbyterianism is Ernest Trice Thompson, *Presbyterians in the South*, 3 vols. (Richmond: John Knox Press, 1963–1973).

Sectional differences, of course, were predicated on the issue of slavery. Albert J. Raboteau's *Slave Religion: The "Invisible Institution" in the Antebellum South* (New York: Oxford University Press, 1978) remains the standard work on African-American religious life. Several works have specifically addressed the issue of Presbyterianism and African-Americans: Andrew E. Murray, *Presbyterians and the Negro—A History* (Philadelphia: Presbyterian Historical Society, 1966); and Gayraud S. Wilmore, *Black and Presbyterian: The Heritage and the Hope* (Philadelphia: Geneva Press, 1983). Finally, C. C. Goen, *Broken Churches, Broken Nation: Denominational Schisms and the Coming of the Civil War* (Macon, Ga.: Mercer University Press, 1985) shows how the denominational divisions among American Protestants, Presbyterians included, anticipated the Civil War.

The formation of Princeton Theological Seminary in 1812 ranks among the most important developments within American Presbyterianism in the nineteenth century. Mark A. Noll has devoted considerable attention to the origins of the seminary, both in *Princeton and the Republic* and in "The Founding of Princeton Seminary," *Westminster Theological Journal* 42 (Fall 1979):72–110. The Princetonians regarded themselves as the defenders of Reformed orthodoxy against the assaults, first, of revival theology and, second, of higher criticism. Biographical sketches of twelve important Princetonians appear in Hugh T. Kerr, ed., *Sons of the Prophets: Leaders in Protestantism from Princeton Seminary* (Princeton, N.J.: Princeton University Press, 1963). Mark Noll offers a useful collection of the Princetonians' own writings in *The Princeton Theology, 1812–1921: Scripture, Science, and Theological Method from Archibald Alexander to Benjamin Warfield* (Grand Rapids: Baker Book House, 1983). Noll also edited *Charles Hodge: The Way of Life*

(New York: Paulist Press, 1987); and Hodge's three-volume *Systematic Theology*, long a staple in conservative seminaries, remains in print even in the final decade of the twentieth century.

Ernest R. Sandeen ("The Princeton Theology: One Source of Biblical Literalism in American Protestantism," *Church History*, 31 [September 1962]:307–321; *The Roots of Fundamentalism: British and American Millenarianism, 1800–1930* [Chicago: University of Chicago Press, 1970]) argues that the Princetonians introduced the notion of biblical inerrancy in the original autographs in 1881, a contention disputed by Randall Balmer in "Princetonians and Scripture: A Reconsideration," *Westminster Theological Journal*, 44 (1982):352–365. What seems indisputable is the pervasive influence of Scottish Common Sense Realism on the Princetonians. See Sydney E. Ahlstrom, "The Scottish Philosophy and American Theology," *Church History* 24 (1955):257–272; Mark A. Noll, "Common Sense Traditions and American Evangelical Thought," *American Quarterly* 37 (1985):216–238; and John C. Vander Stelt, *Philosophy and Scripture: A Study in Old Princeton and Westminster Theology* (Marlton, N.J.: Mack Publishing Co., 1978). On the *Princeton Review*, see Charles H. Lippy, s.v., *"The Princeton Review"* in Charles H. Lippy, ed., *Religious Periodicals of the United States: Academic and Scholarly Journals* (Westport, Conn.: Greenwood Press, 1986).

Princeton's institutional nemesis was Union Theological Seminary in New York, and one of its longtime professors, Robert T. Handy, has distinguished himself as one of the twentieth-century's pre-eminent church historians. Handy's many contributions toward understanding Union and American Protestantism include "Union Theological Seminary in New York and American Presbyterianism, 1836–1904," *American Presbyterians: Journal of Presbyterian History* 66 (Summer 1988):115–122; and *A History of Union Theological Seminary in New York* (New York: Columbia University Press, 1987).

PRESBYTERIANISM IN THE TWENTIETH CENTURY

In many respects the defining event for American Presbyterianism in the twentieth century was the fundamentalist-modernist controversy that raged in the 1920s; its reverberations continue to be felt even in the closing decades of the century. Those who applauded the defeat of the fundamentalists have exulted in a more open and inclusive denomination unfettered by nineteenth-century "orthodox" dogma; see, for example, Lefferts A. Loetscher, *The Broadening Church: A Study of the Theological Issues in the Presbyterian Church since 1869* (Philadelphia: University of Pennsylvania Press, 1954).

On the history of "modernism" among American Protestants, see William R. Hutchison, *The Modernist Impulse in American Protestantism* (Cambridge, Mass.: Harvard University Press, 1976). George M. Marsden has produced what remains the definitive study of the fundamentalist movement, *Fundamentalism and American Culture: The Shaping of Twentieth-Century Evangelicalism, 1870–1925* (New York: Oxford University Press, 1980). One of the key players in the controversy was Harry Emerson Fosdick, pastor of New York's Riverside Church and the subject of a recent biography: Robert Moats Miller, *Harry Emerson Fosdick: Preacher, Pastor, Prophet* (New York: Oxford University Press, 1985). Bradley J. Longfield (*The Presbyterian Controversy: Fundamentalists, Modernists, and Moderates* [New York: Oxford University Press, 1991]) looks at the entire debate from the perspective of its principals.

The fundamentalist spinoffs of the controversy have not received the historiographical attention they deserve. One attempt to redress that is a collection of essays edited by

Charles G. Dennison and Richard C. Gamble: *Pressing Toward the Mark: Essays Commemorating Fifty Years of the Orthodox Presbyterian Church* (Philadelphia: Committee for the History of the Orthodox Presbyterian Church, 1986). Many of the Presbyterian fundamentalists from the controversy of the 1920s later moderated their course and became evangelicals, less strident and militant than the earlier fundamentalists. George Marsden traces this strand within twentieth-century Protestantism (and Presbyterianism) in *Reforming Fundamentalism: Fuller Seminary and the New Evangelicalism* (Grand Rapids: William B. Eerdmans, 1987), in which he sees the formation of Fuller Theological Seminary, with its strong ties to Presbyterianism, as the embodiment of this "neo-evangelicalism."

Missions within the church became a battleground as well, triggered in large part by the so-called Hocking Report, known formally as the Laymen's Foreign Missions Inquiry, The Commission of Appraisal, William Ernest Hocking, Chairman, *Re-Thinking Missions: A Laymen's Inquiry After One Hundred Years* (New York: Harper & Brothers, 1932). Pearl S. Buck's famous responses appeared as "The Laymen's Mission Report," *Christian Century*, 49 (November 23, 1932); and "Is There a Case for Foreign Missions?" *Harper's Monthly Magazine*, 166 (January 1933). Robert E. Speer issued his own measured commentary on the controversial report, *"Re-Thinking Missions" Examined* (New York: Fleming H. Revell, 1933); and a recent study places the entire debate into a much broader context: William R. Hutchison, *Errand to the World: American Protestant Thought and Foreign Missions* (Chicago: University of Chicago Press, 1987).

The attrition of Americans from mainline denominations beginning in the 1960s has provoked a flurry of studies. The most significant by far is Robert Wuthnow, *The Restructuring of American Religion: Society and Faith Since World War II* (Princeton, N.J.: Princeton University Press, 1988). Other books in this genre would include Wade Clark Roof and William McKinney, *American Mainline Religion: Its Changing Shape and Future* (New Brunswick, N.J.: Rutgers University Press, 1987); and William R. Hutchison, ed., *Between the Times: The Travail of the Protestant Establishment in America, 1900–1960* (Cambridge: Cambridge University Press, 1987), which covers an earlier period. R. Stephen Warner's sociological study examines the conflict between evangelicals and liberals on a local level, the Presbyterian church in Mendocino, California: *New Wine in Old Wineskins: Evangelicals and Liberals in a Small-Town Church* (Berkeley and Los Angeles: University of California Press, 1988).

Finally (but not least), a series of six volumes on twentieth-century Presbyterianism was published by Westminster/John Knox Press between 1990 and 1992. The series, edited by Milton J Coalter, John M. Mulder, and Louis B. Weeks, and entitled *The Presbyterian Presence: The Twentieth-Century Experience*, represents the work of numerous scholars, theologians, and clergy on various dimensions of twentieth-century Presbyterianism—piety, missions, evangelism, higher education, theology, polity, finances, attrition, and Presbyterian attitudes on race, gender, and social issues. This ambitious effort, financed by the Lilly Endowment, includes 61 essays and fills nearly 2,000 pages. Although, to paraphrase Edmund S. Morgan's comment about Puritan historiography, these volumes tell us more about twentieth-century Presbyterianism than any sane person should care to know, they are impressive in scope and indispensable to understanding American Presbyterianism.

INDEX

About the Authors

RANDALL BALMER is Associate Professor of Religion at Barnard College, Columbia University. He has published numerous articles in scholarly journals and is the author of *A Perfect Babel of Confusion: Dutch Religion and English Culture in the Middle Colonies* (1989) and *Mine Eyes Have Seen the Glory: A Journey into Evangelical Subculture in America* (1989).

JOHN R. FITZMIER is Associate Dean of Vanderbilt University Divinity School. An authority on American religious history, his special interests include the separation of Church and State and Jonathan Edwards. He has contributed to several books, and his articles have appeared in journals such as the *Religious Studies Review*.